Wasted Youth: Reflections

Wasted Youth: Reflections

James M. Wright

Metamorphic Press

Disclaimer: The following narratives are based on fifty-year-old memories. Riddled with inaccuracies, chronological compressions, liberties, and misdirections, they still convey the gist of experience. My goal has not been to reconstruct the past but to extract its meaning.

Copyright © 2024 by James M. Wright

All rights reserved. No part of this book may be reproduced in any manner whatsoever without written permission except in the case of brief quotations embodied in critical articles and reviews.

First Printing, 2024, by Metamorphic Press, Bath, Maine

CONTENTS

DEDICATION vii

Perspectives 1

1 | Junior Crime 3

2 | Transactions 10

3 | Free Ride 18

4 | Peyote Road 25

5 | Poached Elk & Tarantula 42

6 | Shadow Freight 54

7 | The Subject 67

8 | The Frontier of Flesh & Stone 82

9 | Friction 104

CONTENTS

10 | Unsuitable 113

11 | The Gorge of Despair 123

12 | The Headwaters 213

ACKNOWLEDGMENTS 222
ABOUT THE AUTHOR 224

For Susan

Perspectives

The attributes of liminality or of liminal personae *("threshold people") are necessarily ambiguous, since this condition and these persons elude or slip through the network of classifications that normally locate states and positions in cultural space. Liminal entities are neither here nor there; they are betwixt and between the positions assigned and arrayed by law, custom, convention, and ceremonial.*

Liminal entities, such as neophytes in initiation or puberty rites, may be represented as possessing nothing. They may be disguised as monsters, wear only a strip of clothing, or even go naked, to demonstrate that as liminal beings they have no status, property, insignia, secular clothing indicating rank or role, position in a kinship system—in short, nothing that may distinguish them from their fellow neophytes or initiands. Their behavior is normally passive or humble; they must obey their instructors implicitly, and accept arbitrary punishment without complaint. It is as though they are being reduced or ground down to a uniform condition to be fashioned anew....

Victor Turner, The Ritual Process: Structure and Anti-Structure

Modern technocratic culture does not initiate its young. It does not provide sanctioned experiences whereby young people can pass through the dark night of trial into the freedom and responsibility

of adulthood. It did not officially offer you passageways that were so scary you were forced to light your own fire in order to see. Because true passage rites do not exist, you had to find your own ways of illumining this dark, inward passage....
    Steven Foster and Meredith Little, ***Lost Borders: Coming of Age in the Wilderness***

A poet who begins with a mirror must end with the water of a fountain....
    Gaston Bachelard, ***Water and Dreams: An Essay on the Imagination of Matter*** (translated by Edith R. Farrell)

1

Junior Crime

My career in crime and deviant behavior started with bottle caps, the old-fashioned kind. It was the early 60s, before the era of pull tabs and twist-off containers. At junior high, kids raced through lunch to get outside, the only relief from a day of desk-bound punishment. On the way out, you could buy a drink at the school store. Hundreds of kids poured into the courtyard, eager for sunshine and freedom. What better way to celebrate than by pinching a bottle cap between thumb and middle finger, cocking the hand over your shoulder, and with a snap, propelling the cap smartly through the air? Whoever thought it up was a genius of unintended use. With practice, it'll fly fifty feet or more, whirling like a frisbee. The school administration did not see frisbees; they saw miniature saw blades. "You could put someone's eye out," they said. Soon after kids started doing it, flipping bottle caps was forbidden. Stern announcements crackled over the PA.

Being lost in my own world, I came late to the fad. When I finally mastered the flipping technique at home, I was so excited that I couldn't wait to show off at school. Although I must have heard the announcements, I didn't think they applied to me, only those other people, the kids that got it banned.

As soon as I sent a jagged cap sailing across the courtyard, a recess monitor grabbed me by the arm and marched me down to the vice principal's office. Embarrassed, I listened to the lecture and received the note to take home to my parents. In addition, I had to see Mr. Barnard after school. The vice principal told me this while shaking his head and sighing, perhaps because I'd always been one of the "good kids." This was my first school discipline. I didn't know what to expect, just that the bad boys saw Mr. Barnard after school. I thought it would certainly involve more lecturing, but some of my peers knew better. In whispered confidence, I was informed that the bad boys received "spats."

I'd taken a science class from Mr. Barnard. In the corner near his desk, he'd hung an array of wooden implements that resembled cricket bats. Some of them had holes drilled in the business end. I thought they looked creepy, like something out of a dungeon. But during lessons he ignored them.

When I arrived at Mr. Barnard's room after school, maybe a dozen boys sat in place. These were not the boys I hung out with; these were the boys I avoided. Everyone said they were a bad lot, with their greasy hair and lip-curling sneers. Mr. Barnard called a name and a boy, nodding to his buddies, walked up to the teacher's desk. Knowing what to expect, the boy bent over the desk, resting his weight on his elbows and presenting his bottom. Mr. Barnard selected a thick, holey paddle from his wall of now-frightening implements. "Five spats," he announced. With ritual precision, he applied himself to serving the five blows, each landing with a resounding thwack and accompanied by a wince on the boy's face. I saw right away that the holes enhanced the sting. Mr. Barnard did not go easy on the first boy.

I felt as if roused from a dream. I was going to get spanked, something my parents had only done once or twice, and with their hands, not a weapon. And this insult would be delivered at school, of all places. I quivered.

I watched the parade of boys as they were called to the front of the room. Mr. Barnard checked his list and announced a punishment commensurate with the gravity of each crime. It was an efficient process. You got your spats and returned to your seat to watch your comrades thrashed, reinforcing the lesson not to defy the rules, or that was the idea, anyway. Five was the most anyone got, but I noticed that Mr. Barnard would hit some boys harder than others. When it was my turn, he looked surprised as he called my name. He remembered me from when I took his class. "What are you doing here?" But my crime was printed on his list. He shrugged and motioned for me to bend over the desk. He picked a small paddle and gave me two whacks, neither of which hurt, though the impact jarred me to the quick.

I didn't blame Mr. Barnard, but I rebelled at the procedure. The bad boys kept being bad; it was a lousy deterrent. I must have been the only kid in that classroom that didn't repeat his offense. And my mother would have achieved that result with the simple look she gave me when I got home and I showed her the note she had to sign.

I stayed out of trouble for a couple of years. By fifteen, I had started high school and discovered science fiction fandom with its international network of fanzines, correspondence, and amateur press associations. I asked my parents for a typewriter, and they were pleased to get me one. I read so much it was only logical that I might want to write. Then I asked them for a mimeograph machine, which was kind of weird, but I wanted it badly enough to break down their resistance.

My life changed after that. I came home from school to spend the evenings pounding out letters and fanzines with the energy of a demon. Although this may have appeared harmless enough, I was still the same naive kid, so, I got into trouble.

I belonged to a national fan organization that had a thousand members and published a monthly letterzine, that is, a fanzine consisting entirely of letters written by members. Each issue contained ongoing conversation and commentary where topics could be raised or dropped as letter writers wished. These days it's called social media, but then it was just fandom.

Some guy from Oklahoma wrote an irate letter demanding that all communists should be kicked out of the organization. I couldn't decipher a context for this demand. It didn't strike me as a pressing issue for the membership of a science fiction fan organization, but the author was adamant. He offered no practical suggestions for ferreting out Reds; perhaps he just wanted to make it clear where he stood.

I was immature in many ways, but less so about politics. I'd read some Marx and a little history and knew which end of the political spectrum I preferred. On an impulse, I fired off a letter to the zine proclaiming myself a card-carrying Communist. For good measure, I advocated the violent overthrowal of the government. Take that, Mr. Oklahoma; you can't keep us out; we're already in!

I thought it was a satirical triumph, but it offended a few, including the guy from Oklahoma. Most people ignored it, even if it represented a violation of the Smith Act, the McCarthy era law banning all public declarations of overthrowing the government. The furor died down quickly, though, and I figured the matter laid to rest.

A few weeks later, I was called down to the principal's office. He had a copy of the fanzine with my letter. "What is this?" "It's a fanzine," I said. This irritated him. He waved his finger and told me that the FBI had paid a visit to ask if it was a school publication. That seemed odd to me because the name and address of the organization was printed on the masthead of every issue. "You're in a lot of trouble," he said and sent me back to class.

I dismissed the principal's concern. Who would assume a fanzine was a school publication? Just because it was a crude, mimeographed sheaf of paper? I puzzled over the matter but forgot it by the time I walked home after school. Entering the front door with visions of chocolate chip cookies and milk, I found my parents sitting at either end of our wraparound sofa. This was unusual; they rarely used the sofa at the same time. Perched between them was a man in a suit. He introduced himself as Mr. Clark from the FBI. The blood rushed out of my head. Meekly, I sat down next to him where he patted the cushion.

He also had a copy of the fanzine, open to the page with my letter. No doubt he'd already shown my parents. They sat with frozen expressions; lips so tight they could squeak. Their disappointment was unmistakable.

The federal agent asked me to explain the letter. I'd seen enough tv shows about the feds to imagine that I could be downtown, cuffed to a chair under a glaring lightbulb. In time, I knew I would confess to everything, so I told Mr. Clark why I had written the letter, explaining fandom, fanzines, and all the details of my impulse.

"So," he said, "it was a kind of joke?"

I admitted that it was, or at least that had been the idea. He chuckled, mildly and without humor. "Yes," he said, "that's funny." My parents didn't look like they thought it was funny. At this point, I agreed with them, despite what the agent said.

He nodded with gravity and gave a short speech, commenting that I was an intelligent boy and that our nation needed folks, especially young folks, who could think and write and that I shouldn't be discouraged by this incident but should keep writing. He went on in this vein, leaving me unsure whether I was being investigated or anointed. His praise struck me as disingenuous, but if it scored points with my parents, who were going to kill me as soon as he left, I'd take it.

When he finished, we all stood up together, shook hands around, and saw him to the door. As soon as he left, my parents turned, fixing me in the glare of their headlights. They were furious. But they weren't violent, ever, which is why I'd rarely been spanked at home and not for at least a decade. They didn't know what to say, though. Probably the anger was mixed with confusion and dismay over what a strange child they'd raised. A fifteen-year-old Commie? Where did he come from?

They didn't kill me; they did something even worse. Without a word, they marched into my bedroom. I didn't dare follow. When they came out, my father carried the typewriter in front of him like a contaminated object, and my mother cradled an armload of manuscripts and journals. They said nothing; those things just disappeared. There were no conditions, no ultimatums. I knew better than to raise an objection or ask for leniency. I'd never seen them like that; it was scary.

I don't know if they read my stuff. Probably some of it; I'm sure they were curious. It was mostly bad science fiction and even worse poetry. Nothing radical, though. After a month, my mother gave back the typewriter and the papers. "Here you go," she said.

We never discussed the incident. I know I put them through several varieties of hell with my odd shenanigans, and they got used to having a son who was some kind of rebel. They started paying attention to the political situation in the country, which was hard to ignore if you owned a television or subscribed to a newspaper. The coffins flew back from Vietnam, the sons of friends and neighbors. My father had served in the Coast Guard, but he hated it, and the military. My parents didn't want me to go to Vietnam. They wanted me to stay alive, go to college and do them proud, be a scientist or doctor. Several years later, when I was dodging the draft, I made a quick trip to see them. "Be careful what you say on the phone," my mother told me as if it were neighborhood gossip. "There's a wiretap on it."

2

Transactions

By the time I was a senior in high school, I'd heard about LSD but had no idea how to get my hands on it. No matter how badly I wanted drugs, I lived in a small town in Eastern Washington; if any other kids had access, they kept tight lips about it. I settled for wallpapering my bedroom with psychedelic posters from San Francisco and listened repeatedly to any scrap of recorded acid rock I could find. I lay on my bed and daydreamed about the magic of cerebral chemistry as if it were a pipeline to enlightenment. Sure, I could get beer and wine, but I was unimpressed with the gateway stuff. I wanted cosmic shit, full bore.

After graduating from high school in 67, I went to Seattle to attend the University of Washington. By the time I checked in to the dorm, I'd lost interest in studying philosophy. I attended classes for a week before walking out of my dorm and into the streets. I wanted to be a hippie. I didn't think about it, I just traded in my old life. There was no adjustment period between bourgeois suburbia and psychedelic wilderness, between straight kid and stoner freak. I turned on and dropped out. Like everyone else in the scene, I now lived in the jungle of the black market, the unlicensed pharmacy of the streets. I soon learned that consumers and dealers were often the same people and the best way to keep yourself high was to sell the product. I was hungry, so I did what I had to do; the fact that it was a crime just made it more interesting.

It turned out that I was a lousy drug dealer. I failed to make money and I did bad things. For success, you had to be sharp, enterprising, and ruthless—in other words, a rock-hard capitalist. Not really my skill set. Still, you couldn't immerse yourself in the drug scene without getting involved in transactions. And I was immersed. From morning till night, you would find me on the crowded streets of the University District, or on the park-like periphery of campus known as Hippie Hill. From The Hill you could sit on the lawn and overlook the throngs of idlers milling around 42nd Street, the heart of the scene. It was a magnet for the kids from the suburbs and anyone else wanting acid, speed, or grass. If you stood around and looked like you belonged, you'd soon be asked if you had anything for sale. If you knew someone who was holding, you'd be happy to make the connection. Or maybe you were holding a stash for a buddy. No matter how the deal went down, it went down.

Confusion proliferated on 42nd Street and the adjacent blocks of University Avenue. There were so many people wandering the sidewalks and leaning up against the buildings that it must have been hard for the narcs to sort out who was doing what. When cop cars showed up, people drifted away; when the police moved on, the scene reassembled itself. Undercover agents stood out like sore thumbs, were quickly identified, and openly mocked. It took the police awhile to figure out how to deal with the hippies; these new freaks didn't function like the previous generations of drug dealers. They believed in the free market, the purest form of unregulated commerce, but they turned it into a festival. People wore flamboyant clothes, grew tons of hair, preened like renaissance fops, and gave out free samples because it was fun and good for business, too. One evening somebody slipped through the crowd passing out amyl nitrite poppers; before long 42nd Street was a seething mass of stoned hippies, hundreds of them. The streetlights got busted and freaks careened from curb to curb in the darkness, a sort of proto-mosh pit. The cops never showed up; wisely, they let it die out on its own. The next day, people and things were back in their places.

I spent most of my time on the Ave leaning against walls and parked cars with my red-haired high-school friend Kid Carrot and his buddy Maniac. When a potential customer walked by, which could be anyone they didn't know, one of them caught an eye and barked "acid, grass, speed." Mostly that's what people wanted. Sometimes there were guys, usually rail-thin, looking for crystal. That meant crystal methedrine, an injectable speed that fucked you up like nothing else on the streets. Both Carrot and Maniac had shot crystal for a couple of years before burning out. They wanted nothing to do with it. I helped them however I could: errands, holding, deliveries, solicitation, whatever. As a result, I had acid and grass for myself, as much as I wanted. I took their advice and stayed away from the speed.

Many dealers stashed their product in the bushes on Hippie Hill, so they didn't have to hold the contraband. You contacted a customer on the street and took them up to the lawn; while they sat and counted their cash, you ducked into the shrubs to grab a lid. A lid was a bag of marijuana, supposedly an ounce, but usually less than that. A Baggie brand plastic sandwich bag served as the standard container, rolled up and tucked into its own flap. A dozen or so lids could be packed into a shopping bag and stashed under a carpet of leaves. Because it was all part of the Hippie good vibe, people didn't work too hard to hide the dope. It needed to be handy, that was the point, yet still far enough away to disavow ownership if the cops showed up.

Somebody, I don't remember who, got the idea of raiding these stashes, many of which were left overnight. First thing in the morning, we'd slink around like cartoon crooks, combing the foliage, searching for drugs. We found stuff and we sold it as fast as possible. Clearly, this was a violation of the Hippie Code, but I don't remember any ethical deliberation on our part. We knew we didn't want to get caught, that seemed the primary concern. For a few weeks, we made some easy money, then everybody got wise and stopped hiding stuff in the bushes. My best theft, if that's the right adjective, was finding a small duffle with about twenty lids, a baggie of speed tabs, and a .32 automatic pistol. I ran straight to Carrot and showed him my loot. "Jesus," he said, and took the pistol, which he sold within five minutes without leaving the hill. Somebody else bought all the speed and we sold off the lids one by one. The gun changed everything, though. Suddenly, the enterprise seemed a lot more dangerous. I don't know how we got away with these heists without getting the shit kicked out of us, if not shot. We didn't brag about it, so maybe nobody figured out where their dope went missing. Plus, that's how the free market works: dog eat dog.

Grass made up most of the product sold on the streets. People smoked it like tobacco, in skinny joints passed from hand to hand like a sacrament; it epitomized the vibe, the ethos that everyone wanted, or thought they did. In those days, the quality of marijuana covered a large spectrum, from the three-toke high of Acapulco Gold to the foggy buzz of chain-smoked leaf that claimed no origin. If you had good stuff, you made smaller lids. The price was the same: ten bucks a lid. You didn't change the price; you adjusted the contents. If customers complained, you shrugged your shoulders; there were other customers.

One day a friend of Maniac's returned from a road-trip to the Midwest. He raved about finding weed growing along the highways of Kansas. He'd filled the trunk of his car with it. We walked around the block and inspected his find. Indeed, it was marijuana, or hemp, to be precise. We took garbage bags of this stuff to the laundromat and ran them through the dryer, which cooked the leaves down to a crinkly texture. We rolled and smoked a joint. It tasted like weed. We smoked another one. After four or five joints, no one was high, though we all had a little buzz from inhaling so much smoke. Good enough. We filled baggies of the stuff and sold them on the street. The baggies were plump and inviting in appearance. We told everybody the same thing. "It's not your high test, man, but it's pot." People's eyes bugged out at the size of the lids. It was a great deal, cheapest marijuana on the street. Some fools even came back for more.

This operation seemed like free money, but it was a long way to Kansas. So, we drove out of Seattle and down rural backroads, harvesting whatever green plants might fill the bill. We went back to the laundromat, dried and packaged the stuff, whatever it was, and sold it, too. It's amazing how nobody complained. You just tell them up front, "Yeah, it's not the best, but hey, you're getting good count."

The hippie scene declined swiftly, its idealism discarded among the rip offs, drug deaths, psychedelic casualties, and trashed fields of rock festivals. Within nine months of my arrival on the scene, most of the people I knew were into heroin. Including Carrot and Maniac. No longer were they fun to be around. Instead, they spent their days slumped into chairs in that dying grandfather pose common to junkies, whining about imaginary ailments until they nodded out. When they weren't loaded, they jabbered about copping the next fix. Carrot and Maniac respected my lack of interest, protecting me like big brothers, but other friends kept promising to turn me on, "You don't have to shoot it, man, just snort a few lines, you'll see." Of course, once they copped, it was far too precious to waste on novices. I didn't insist, not after the hundredth time of sitting in a dim room watching them cook the heroin to a liquid in a metal spoon, draw it into a syringe, tie off their bicep with a belt, then fire straight into a vein. If they could find one that wasn't collapsed. Eventually, all the spoons in the kitchen had burnt bottoms.

I fled Seattle and took my first trip to the Bay Area, to Oakland, where I knew somebody from science fiction fandom. I asked him if I could pay a visit because an old buddy from high school was now at USC and had written to say that if I could get as far as the Bay Area, he'd come up and front me a gram of acid. A gram of acid was a lot of acid. In those days, the standard dose was 250 micrograms. Four thousand hits in a gram. At five bucks a hit, that's get-rich-quick territory, even after paying back the front. I was more than tired of being broke, so I begged a ride to Oakland with a guy I'd met on the streets, a musician. I didn't really know him, he wasn't a friend, and after a while, I was glad of that. He talked too much about pubescent girls; not my idea of a fun road trip conversation between men. He was a creep, but I kept my mouth shut; in those days you weren't supposed to bum anyone's trip. Besides, it was a ride.

I stayed in Oakland longer than I expected. I kept calling my friend in LA about the acid. He wasn't sure when, he said. He was working on it. I'd told my host that I only needed to stay for a few days. Nearly penniless, I filled my time wandering the streets of Berkeley or I sat on the couch in the living room and read from the gargantuan library. After a month of this, my host got tired of the situation and politely asked me to leave. By that point, I figured there wasn't going to be a gram of acid, anyway. Nothing unusual about this kind of transaction in the drug scene, an imaginary connection with a fabulous offer. You could spend a lot of time and energy talking about these schemes, as if a volume of words would help them materialize.

I hitch-hiked back to Seattle, where I moved into an abandoned station wagon parked in the alley behind a café. I solicited spare change on the street and each day ate one twenty-five-cent peanut butter and jelly sandwich from the café. By that time, the drug scene in the U District was oriented to the heroin trade. Those foolish enough to shop for mere weed or acid often ended up with product that had been stepped on so many times it was a shadow of itself. Or sometimes, the customer got totally burned: the dealer went around the corner and never came back. People got assaulted over rip offs, and the burn artists specializing in selling nothing could often be seen on the street with new sets of bruises and bandages. I spent more time sitting in the café, reading or watching chess, avoiding the pallor overwhelming my friends. The psychedelic street festival was over, replaced by a darker carnival, a freak show of survival. With reckless abandon, we had all contributed to the transformation, putting our shoulders to the tumbrel of self-destruction.

3

Free Ride

The guy turned out to be a reckless bastard, but as a hitchhiker, how was I supposed to know? It's a ride; you take it. He picked me up outside the Bay Area on US 99; said he was going to Seattle. That worked. I'd been in Berkeley for a month and my welcome had worn thin. Back in Seattle there'd be places to crash, but I had to get there. I didn't have much experience at hitchhiking, and this was my first solo. It hadn't gone well, taking hours to get out of the urban sprawl. When the guy said he'd take me the rest of the way, I thought I had it made.

By 1968, Interstate 5 still had a few incomplete sections, including a stretch through northern California covered by the two-lane US 99. It's easier to solicit rides when you can stand on the shoulder; drivers see you at a distance and give you a thought. On ramps are a bitch; traffic is accelerating and there's usually nowhere to stop. Experienced travelers told me I had better get a ride along 99 going the full distance or I'd be screwed. A short haul could leave you stranded somewhere like Roseburg,

Oregon, a logging town where no one would pick you up and the cops cruised past over and over.

I held a sign that said "Seattle," but time and cars flowed by. Hours later, a Ford Galaxie passed me, slowed down and pulled over. I ran in pursuit and hopped in. The driver had short hair, wore a button shirt, and slacks; I thought he might be a traveling businessman. He handed me a pint of cheap whiskey and peeled out. He said his name and I said mine, but we didn't shake hands; the whiskey was enough.

The Drunk liked to drive fast. It made me nervous, so I nipped at the whiskey and said nothing, giving the guy the benefit of the doubt. Hey, it was a ride all the way to Seattle, you don't mess with that. We talked, but it was shit-shooting, worthless chat. He asked some questions but didn't listen to the answers. I was just an anchor for the passenger seat, somebody to share the booze and listen to his blather.

About half the bottle of whiskey disappeared and we roared along, living the freedom of the road. Suddenly, we came up behind a line of four or five cars following a slow truck. A farmer, maybe. The Drunk pounded on the steering wheel and swore, took another swig from the bottle, thrust it at me, and swerved into the other lane. He stepped on it, because he was passing the whole line; there wasn't anywhere to squeeze in. He got us past one car, then we saw a line of traffic coming the other way, straight at us. We were trapped. Shit, he said. He stomped on the gas pedal and the car leaped forward. I assumed that I was going to die. However, nobody else on the road wanted to die, certainly not in a ten-car cataclysm, so the oncoming traffic nudged toward the shoulder. The line of cars we were passing did the same thing. The Drunk, full blast shot the gap, right down the center line.

As soon as he could, he jerked the car back into its lane, and reached over for the booze. He laughed and asked if I was scared.

"Yes," I whispered.

He drained the bottle and tossed it in the back. Reaching under the driver's seat, he produced a fresh one. A different brand, but still cheap whiskey. What was I to do? I could have insisted on getting out, but I didn't have an ounce of agency; I was just along for the free ride. He handed me the bottle, and I took another drink. Fuck, we almost bought it. He didn't say anything more about the close call and acted as if it never happened, yet he did ease off a tad. He was still going too fast and drinking too much, but death didn't seem imminent, or maybe I was just getting used to it.

The miles rolled by, then it got dark. We'd made it to the interstate, four lanes of divided, limited access highway. At least you could pass without risking a head-on collision. Somewhere in southwestern Washington, he suddenly drove on to the shoulder and stopped. The Drunk wanted a nap. He said I should crawl into the back seat; he'd take the front. I did what he said, thinking, shit we were almost there. I shoved the empties into the footwell. Too many to count; it looked like all his road trips involved benders.

I wrapped my coat around me and soon fell asleep. It was still dark when I awoke to a sharp tapping on the window. A state policeman, with a flashlight, peered in. The Drunk could have taken an exit and pulled onto a side road or somewhere out of the way, but he didn't do that, he pulled over on the shoulder of a major interstate highway. Of course, the cops checked it out.

Under arrest, we sat in the back of the patrol car, saying nothing, while the cop drove to the nearest town, Centralia, Washington. I'd never been there, but I'd read about it; it was famous in labor history. In 1919, there had been a riot on the streets of Centralia between vigilantes of the American Legion and activists with the IWW, the Wobblies. Six people, mostly Legionnaires, were killed that day. In retribution, a mob of locals stormed the jail, removed a Wobbly, and lynched him from the bridge. Ever since, it's been known as the Centralia Massacre, or the Centralia Tragedy, depending on whose side you're on. As far as I knew, Centralia was still a bad-ass place unwelcoming to leftists, hippies, or bohemians. I fit into all those categories.

After we got to the police station, they took The Drunk through a door; I never saw him again. Two officers escorted me to an empty cell and locked me in. It was my first time. Stark and cold like I expected, at least I was alone instead of crammed in with a bunch of rednecks. A couple hours of sitting on a bunk and I sobered up. After dawn, they served me an institutional breakfast.

Later in the morning, I was taken to see a judge. He made no mention of my grubby clothes, long, stringy hair, and general derelict appearance. Instead, he named the charge: a minor in possession of alcohol. I pled guilty. "You've served a little time," he said, "so I'm going to let you go. If you get picked up again for drinking or hitchhiking, I'll make you wish you'd never heard of Centralia. Now get out of here."

I left the jail and walked into a typical western Washington day: overcast, threat of drizzle, gloomy. I had no money, not a single coin. Seattle was still a hundred miles north. I couldn't hitch and the passenger train cost five bucks. I didn't have any idea how I was supposed to get home. At the time, the idea of home included crashpads, which was all I had waiting. Unfortunately, none of these friends had a phone, or even a car to come get me. I started wandering around the streets of Centralia.

It wasn't long before a cruiser rolled past in slow motion. I ignored it, but it was a solid reminder that I shouldn't try hitching, begging, or loitering. Few people were out on the streets; the prospects for bumming spare change looked non-existent, anyway. It was a quiet town, a mill town; workers were at work and housewives kept house.

I walked by a Protestant church; I don't remember which flavor. Driven by a sudden inspiration, I walked up the steps and through the door. Nobody home, just God. Austere, like most Protestant churches, boring. Then I saw the collection box in front of the pulpit. Why not take a look, I thought. A simple box with a lid, protected by reverence. I opened it and took out the change, a little over a dollar. Not enough, but I perceived a method. There were other churches.

I walked the streets, looking for opportunities. My system was simple: if the church door was unlocked, I'd go in and scan for a cash repository. If someone asked me what I was doing, I'd say I was seeking solace during hard times, which was true. Nothing need be said about my lack of religion, prayer, belief, or any other quality that tied me to the practice of Christianity. I'd been raised a Protestant, sort of. My mother took me and my sister to church until I was old enough to express reluctance. She then insisted that I sample several other churches in town, including the Catholic. I didn't like them; I'd rather stay home and read. When I turned ten, she gave up and nobody went to church. Except once a year we went to the sunrise Easter service at the local drive-in theater where we could stay in our pajamas and curl up in the back seat under a blanket. I was okay with that; I could bring a book.

In Centralia, I had no comforts, not even a book, and I felt lost. After the initial windfall, I tried several more churches for no gain. Finally, at a locked church, when I knocked on the door, the pastor opened it. I asked for a job, anything I could do to earn the money for a train ticket. I gave him an edited version of my story, emphasizing misfortune. He asked if I could trim hedges. I could, actually, having done so for my father as part of the family allowance scam. The pastor told me to wait on the steps while he fetched a pair of shears. He then pointed to the hedges on the church lawn.

They didn't need trimming, but I touched them up here and there as best I could, exercising restraint so I didn't butcher anything. I went at it for an hour or so. Then it started to rain because it rains nearly every day in Centralia. No way the rain was going to interfere with my ticket out of town, so I kept at it, smartly clipping branches. Eventually, the pastor could take no more of my pathetic endeavor, opened the door and waved me in.

He led me through the church and into his study, which looked like every other pastor's study that I'd seen, even the ones on television. Books, chairs, desk, papers, file cabinets, crosses, bibles, sad honky Jesus pictures on the wall, all the basic gear.

He asked me to sit, and he handed me a cup of hot chocolate, plus the five dollars. Then we talked. He turned out to be a nice guy and exerted no energy toward recruiting. We just chatted, and he asked questions about where I was from and what I was doing with my life. I don't remember what I said, but since I'd only dropped out of my philosophy major the previous year, I probably came up with something that passed for an existential justification.

He gave me a ride to the train station in time to catch the afternoon run to Seattle. As the train rocked and clattered along, I stared out the rain-streaked window at intervals of forest and industry. I wondered about freedom, having it, losing it, telling the difference. Everything was free, in a way. A ride on the highway, food and lodging in jail, church money, hot chocolate, a train ticket. I was getting a free ride through life. Or maybe it was a free fall.

4

Peyote Road

Late in the summer of 68, three of us fled the grim streets of Seattle and drove to New Mexico. All over the country, people talked about going back to the land, whatever that meant. Dick wanted to kill an elk, and Kid Carrot knew people in the hills of northern New Mexico, but me, I was along for the lark. I'd met Carrot's friends on the streets and heard the legends; they were hard-edged and charismatic, the trendsetters. After the hallucinogens and speed burned everyone out, they moved on to heroin. Things got heavier with junk; its gravity weighed you down; you talked in whispers and slunk through shadows, cool and important. Fear kept me from it. For one thing, there was the needle. They said that those afraid of needles made the best junkies, but I couldn't get past the terror of stabbing myself to insert a liquid death-in-life, not even for the bliss. No, I wanted psychedelic rainbows and cosmic visions.

A few days of driving brought us to Vallecitos, a rustic hamlet at nine thousand feet tucked into rolling hills of pine and juniper. Carrot's friends lived in a three-room wooden shack on the only street, a dirt road. A dozen other houses, mostly adobe, a dilapidated church, and a closet-sized post office comprised the town. Until our friends had moved in, the population had been 100% Latino. The locals scratched a living from the earth, never a lucrative enterprise, so when hippies wanted to rent an empty house, they were happy to take the money. Five dollars per room was the going rate. Wood fueled the stoves for heating and cooking, water had to be pumped by hand, and the outhouse required negotiations with black widow spiders. It was the antithesis of how I grew up, closer to the Depression-era childhood that my parents had worked so hard to leave behind. Ignoring the hardships of the previous generation, we called our lifestyle "funky," thought we were full of soul, and dressed our parts like a cross between Wild West outlaws and Bloomsbury bohemians.

The house belonged to Tubbs and Drone and their "old ladies," Wendy and Mickey. Other people floated in and out, including people who had come under scrutiny of the Seattle Narcotics Squad and needed to lose the heat, people with names like Smelly, Rufus, and Rubio. Most of the visitors did not bring women, leaving Wendy and Mickey, or whoever was current, with the household labor. That was the essential part of being an old lady, that, and sex. The men ignored the inequities and did men things, like get loaded and swap bullshit.

Carrot, Dick, and I slept upstairs in the attic with the spiders, a nerve-wracking assignment made feasible after drinking enough Coors. All it takes is one time waking up and spotting a black widow advancing over the top of your sleeping bag before you start inspecting every square inch of bedding at regular intervals through the night. That is, if you can rouse yourself out of the torpor of cheap beer.

I said I came to Vallecitos on a lark, which explains nothing. I tagged along because that's what I knew how to do. I relied on others to get me high, and I took what was offered. Although they talked about turning me on to heroin, I never pushed. I knew it was just talk. Fine by me. I smoked weed, dropped acid, and when I could find it, I consumed psilocybin, hashish, and the fabled super-drug STP. And alcohol, of course, the great mixer. Mescaline, however, eluded me. I considered this a shortcoming in my resume. I'd read Huxley and bought in to the mystique. Even though I'd swallowed capsules called mescaline, they were weak and unconvincing, hardly mythic. Like so much else on the street market in those days, probably a scam.

Tubbs and Drone told me they'd taken peyote, the cactus that contained mescaline, and not that long ago. They said it was cool. You'll get some soon, they assured me, people brought it up from Mexico and Texas all the time. But they weren't invested in tracking it down. They had the itch for heroin, tried to dampen it with booze, or anything, really. None of which worked, and certainly not mescaline.

I'd been there for a week or so when Rufus arrived from Seattle, driving a Cadillac with fins that belonged on a shark. We helped him unload an old-fashioned trunk, which he motioned for us to carry inside while he looked around to make sure we weren't observed. Safe from the eyes of chance, he opened it. Like a master of ceremonies, he pulled out one oriental rug after another, each more fabulous than the last. Even to an untrained eye, the quality was obvious. Rufus, beaming with mischief, unfurled the largest one, an exquisite Persian weave, worth ten grand at least, he said. I figured the rugs were hot. Rufus wouldn't say, he just gave us a show incorporating all the jerky gestures, tics, and odd, angular poses peculiar to his overtaxed nervous system. On the streets, he and I had exchanged a few polite words in mutual company, but I didn't know him as a friend. Everyone talked about him with a kind of awe; he was mysteriously weird. As a dealer, he had access to large quantities and, according to Carrot, had diverted a whole gram of LSD for a personal experiment, dosing himself every day for a year, increasing the dose as needed to maintain the high. Since then, he'd become a twitching machine, dancing with dyskinesia. Now he was into heroin, perhaps a calming agent after the jangly acid carnival.

At first, the rugs decorated the interior walls of the Vallecitos shack, a counterpoint of riches in the rustic. This lasted for a couple of weeks, then they were bundled up and taken south. Tubbs, Drone, and Rufus could no longer resist. They sold the rugs to a fence in Albuquerque and drove across the border to Juarez, where heroin could be purchased openly in shooting galleries. Pay your money, get your dope and works, fire up, then lay around and fondle prostitutes or yourself or just the fabric on the couch. Textures were a big part of the high, which is why junkies liked leather, satin, velvet, and silk. Many times, I'd watched those guys shoot dope and nod off on the sofa, stroking the fabric of their garments as if it was the skin of a lover.

They were gone for a few days, leaving the house in our care. Dick went off in the woods, armed to the teeth, hunting for big game. No one understood why he did this. We talked about living off the land, but never did anything about it. Getting loaded was more important. Dick, apparently, had his own ideas. Mickey paid a long visit to another lover in the nearby town of El Rito. This left me, Carrot, and Wendy, which was fine. One of the El Rito hippies dropped by and left us a bandanna knotted around a handful of fresh peyote buttons. We decided not to wait for the junkies to get back. Fuck them, they're not here, that was the sentiment.

Fresh peyote is rare; for transport and consumption it's commonly dried into wrinkled, brown chips the consistency of tree bark. In the original state, the dome-shaped cactus measures two to four inches in diameter, a bubble of blue-green flesh hugging the ground, flowering annually with delicate pink or white petals. A slow-growing desert plant, it takes years to mature. Twenty-eight alkaloids are produced inside the button, the most notorious of which is mescaline. It grows nowhere in the world except southern Texas and northern Mexico. For more than five thousand years, indigenous people have harvested and eaten the little cactus, incorporating it into culture, religion, and ritual. It took until the 1800s for white folks to discover it and decide that they wanted it, too, like everything else the natives had.

Setting out a plate with six buttons, we took turns slicing off bite-sized chunks. We chewed, aghast at the taste. The flesh was bitter, insanely bitter, and each bite released alkaloid juices that deviled the taste buds. It was like nothing else. We choked it down, chasing each bite with a swig of Coors. Many people vomit after eating peyote, without apparently diminishing the effects. Some say it enhances them. I'm not sure how anyone knows either way. We grimaced and groaned but held it in.

When we finished the chore of masticating and swallowing what we all agreed was the worst thing we'd ever eaten, Carrot said, "I'd eat shit if it got me high." We laughed, but the thought crossed my mind that shit might have been easier.

I put an album on the turntable, an old recording of The Swan Silvertones, the most elegant of the Southern acapella gospel groups. As mellow harmonies filled the room, Carrot drifted to one end of the couch. Wendy and I migrated to the other end, sitting close. I'd been nursing a crush on her, but because she was with Tubbs, I kept it to myself. Being simple, I thought that's what you were supposed to do. The music smoothed over all the rough edges as the peyote flooded our nervous systems. Colors soon seemed brighter, geometric patterns appeared where once had been blank walls, and my muscles oozed into soup. Wendy and I held hands, our heads drifted into a nuzzle, and we melted together, entranced. It was sensual, yet chaste, like floating away on a cloud for two.

We spent the night in rapture, listening to the record play over and over, while time, sound, and space merged into a stretched moment of being. Indigenous legend says that the peyote cactus will come home with you if you play your music. Given the celestial vibe, we must have pleased it well.

The boys came back from Juarez a few days later. Their first task involved downing a laxative so they could shit out the heroin-filled balloons they'd swallowed in Mexico. Then it was back to business, shooting up and nodding out. Rufus left for Seattle so he could make more money. It would have been a ride for me, but I stuck around, hoping for more peyote. Soon, Tubbs said, though I figured he didn't care. He now had Wendy with him in heroin la-la land and they were on cloud nine. I had no right to be annoyed, but I wanted her to prefer the psychedelic path. Sadly, as if it didn't happen, we never mentioned the night of peyote bliss.

One afternoon a Chevy sedan pulled onto the gravel in front of the house. The driver was a guy named Gilberto, accompanied by three Latino friends. They didn't get out of the car, just rolled down the windows. We leaned against the doors or fenders and passed them Coors. A lit joint was handed back. This was how they always visited; I rarely saw them get out of the car. We'd spend an hour or two exchanging stories. A lot of banter, like you might expect, but not always. Sometimes it was political. Most of Gil's friends were radicals carrying an old grudge. The 1848 Treaty of Guadalupe Hidalgo ended the Mexican American War and put the Southwest under US control. As part of that, Mexican nationals residing in the annexed territories were supposed to receive permanent land grants for their properties. In typical American fashion, grants were often ignored, and land was taken, sold, or distributed to Anglos. More than a century later, many Latinos were fed up and, in the spirit of the 60s civil rights movements, they organized. At first, the movement was peaceful. Reies Tijerina ran for governor from the new Alianza Party. He lost. Regardless, the feds, paranoid as usual, monitored the movement, suspicious of the revolutionary rhetoric. Frustrated with the lack of political progress and angry as federal indictments and arrests were enacted against leaders of the Alianza, they decided on direct action. One day in 1967, a group descended on the Tierra Amarilla County Courthouse to release jailed Alianza comrades and perform a citizen's arrest of the District Attorney who'd jailed them. Channeling the legacy of Pancho Villa, they wore sombreros, crisscross bandoliers, cowboy boots, and were heavily armed. The attorney wasn't there, but two police were wounded in the shoot-out as the radicals freed their colleagues and fled into the hills.

Tijerina had been identified at the raid, and soon thousands of National Guard troops with tanks and armored personnel carriers combed the byways of northern New Mexico in a massive manhunt. To calm things down, Tijerina and a few others eventually surrendered. A year passed without a trial. During that time, the key witness against the Alianza turned up dead in a ditch. As the conflict transitioned into the legal arena, the remaining raiders dispersed back into their communities and tried to shed the heat. One of those was our friend Gil. He pointed out a guy in the back seat, a kid no older than me. "That's Moises," he said, "out on bail, pending on five hundred counts. He was at TA." We exchanged nods with Moises, impressed. If you were at the Tierra Amarilla raid, you were automatically one heavy motherfucker. It was macho royalty, and people respected you, because there was popular support for the land grant movement. And even those who didn't support the movement, well, few were dumb enough to antagonize the Alianza dudes.

Gil got out of the car to open the trunk. An embroidered sombrero sat on top of a gray blanket. I wondered about the lumps under the blanket. Rumor had it that these guys always traveled with a small arsenal, but I wasn't going to ask. Gil picked up the sombrero, turned it in his hands with admiration, and presented it to Tubbs. "Keep it, man. It's cool. I wore it at TA."

We passed it around and everyone tried it on. It was heavy and stiff, a serious hat. Absolutely not my style.

Gil liked the idea of hippies, but most of them were too soft, he said. We escaped this judgment, perhaps because we dressed and talked like outlaws, drank Coors, and shot junk. We'd never be mistaken for flower children. When Gil explained their revolution, we didn't wince but cheered him on. One day, talking politics, Gil surprised me. "People accuse us of being communists," he said. "Hell yes, we're communists!" For him, there was no other way to be. Somehow, we'd been incorporated into his view of what constitutes a comrade. We shared our food, drugs, booze, and banter, and he did the same. Sometimes he came over with a woman he called his girlfriend, a voluptuous Latina wearing the tightest imaginable clothes, so tight she could hardly move. He said, proudly, that she was a "nympho" and would do us all. I don't know if any of the others took her up on that. Maybe, they were always horny, or so it seemed to me, still shy about these things. When Gil brought the girlfriend, I faded into the background. It was too crude for my taste, not that I even had a handle on what constituted my taste. Despite my innocence, or maybe because of it, the whole idea of a woman as a commodity shared among men left me uneasy and insecure. It wasn't romantic like eating peyote, listening to gospel music, and snuggling through the night.

Rufus returned from Seattle on a motorcycle, a chopped Harley. Shortly after, Smelly and his buddy White showed up, and the little shack became too crowded. Carrot, Dick, and I rented an empty adobe house about a hundred yards away on the other side of the valley watercourse. It ran dry much of the year, and it was easy to walk back and forth over rocks and through the weeds, shorter than following the road around.

The locals didn't show any overt displeasure about the hippie boom. Soon after we moved into the new house, our next-door neighbor Mañuel invited us over for dinner, an awkward evening spent around the kitchen table eating beans and tortillas made by his wife. We chatted with Mañuel while the wife and kids ate silently, looking at us like envoys from another planet. They were the latest of half a dozen generations of peasants who had lived on this land, growing their gardens, keeping some livestock, piecing together life season after season. We were, what? Tourists, at best. "Anglos."

We spent our days hanging out with Tubbs and the guys at the shack and marched back to our place for dinner. The trail through the brush was narrow and we walked single file. One day, Mañuel, out tending his garden, motioned me over. "I see you," he said. "You are always at the back. You follow behind, quiet, say nothing. But you watch, you see." I searched his eyes for some sign of mockery or admonishment, but it wasn't there. He announced a simple fact of observation, the testimony of a witness. He wasn't asking me to be different, just letting me know that he noticed. I was too stunned to say anything, so I just nodded and smiled. He smiled back, satisfied, and returned to weeding his corn. Of course, he was right. I watched others, yet my self-awareness was minimal. After he said that, I couldn't get it out of my head.

Following weeks of nothing but booze and weed, we heard a rumor that a batch of peyote had arrived at the Hog Farm commune near El Rito. It was fresh, they said, straight from the desert of Laredo. And they were throwing a party. Piling into vehicles, most of us went, not only in the hope of magic cactus, but because the Hog Farm was a magnet for women.

The commune started in Southern California in the mid-60s as a social experiment. When asked, they categorized themselves as a "mobile, hallucination-extended family." Led by a clown named Wavy Gravy, they eventually gained fame at Woodstock where they were hired to provide security. Taking a novel approach, they formed the Please Police, influencers who politely asked people to stop antisocial behaviors, and offered suggestions for what to do instead. Wherever they went they hosted festive gatherings and gave away food and drugs, all in the name of promoting peace and love. New Mexico had a history of harboring bohemians, so it was a logical destination for the nomadic Hog Farm entourage.

I arrived at the party curious but wary. Clowns made me paranoid. The masked persona was too volatile and too ill-defined for my social insecurities. Wavy Gravy was no exception. As he swept through the encampment in his weird costume, festooned with stars and a jester's cowl, he dispensed pranks and cheer. Most people seemed to find him amusing, responding with a giggle, a hug, or a hit of reefer. Not me; I stayed the hell away. I wanted the peyote, but not from him.

Maybe a hundred people milled around, wandering through the open geodesic dome, gathering food from the trencher table piled with wholesome dishes, drinking wine and beer, smoking dope, dancing to drums and flutes, the usual. I sat on the periphery with a paper plate full of beans and rice and watched my friends sniff out women like prowling wolves. I followed their progress from a safe distance, admiring their ease with strangers. I never learned how to party; the circumstances baffled me. Small talk eluded my attention span, and I didn't understand the first thing about flirting. It all felt like a performance without a script and failed to lure me out of anxious withdrawal. At parties, I'd learned to intoxicate myself until it was over, a form of endurance. Maybe one of my friends would score some peyote and share it with me.

Some people are drawn to wallflowers; they want to rescue them. Psychotics, evangelists, and altruists are all keen to fill this role, in my experience. And before I could even finish my beans and rice, a beaming young woman sauntered over and sat on the bench beside me. She had that floral hippie beauty: long brown hair, a paisley skirt, a loose blouse that suggested everything, and the glowing skin of a goddess. "Want to get high?" she asked. Of course I did, I always did. She lit a joint and handed it to me. I inhaled reverently, as one should, and exploded in coughing. There was weed in the joint, but there was something else, something acrid and harsh. I inhaled again and handed it back. Within seconds, swirling geometries of color spun in my eyes, announcing a psychedelic rush. "Holy shit," I said. The beneficent one smiled at me, and I felt the calling of true love. "Peyote," she said. She reached into a leather pouch strung to her waist and pulled out a foil-wrapped chunk. Inside the foil rested a black ball of tar. She carefully tore off a thumbnail-sized piece and placed it in my palm. "Take it for later. We boiled down the buttons," she said. "It's concentrated." But I already knew that, reeling from the knockout punch of two puffs, the equivalent of who knew how many buttons.

I wanted her to stay with me forever, so we could take the yellow brick road to mescaline heaven, but I was so stoned that I didn't even ask her name, just grinned like a stump. She smiled and in a final blessing before walking away, gave me the rest of the joint.

I sat on the bench and held my own party. Rufus came over and I gave him a hit. "Jesus Christ," he said, a benediction from the psychedelic veteran. He handed the joint back to me, but I waved it away. I needed nothing more from life. The goddess had visited and blessed me. Bored with my trance, he wandered off, waving the joint like a conductor's wand.

I kept my place on the bench and studied the changing colors of the sky. No matter the hour, I found them remarkable. When daylight started to fade, Rufus reappeared. "Hey, let's bolt. I need to get back before dark. You've been wanting a ride on the bike."

I didn't remember saying I wanted to ride on his bike, the chopper he'd acquired in some kind of drug trade. Out of politeness, I might have indicated that'd be nice, one of those things you say to be pleasant, secure in the knowing that it would never come up again. The bike was a loud and obnoxious piece of machinery, and I wanted no part of it. Rufus talked like he was doing me a favor, though, and I didn't want to be ungrateful, so I went along.

The road from El Rito to Vallecitos was a curvy, winding road, and climbed a thousand feet over twenty miles, a scenic route through arid hills. As we roared out of the Hog Farm camp, Rufus announced, "Damn headlight doesn't work. We need to jet. Hang tight, I'm steppin' to it." I clung to the seat and leaned into him, listening to the hum of peyote in my head. Rufus sped around the turns, angling into the corners, and I gripped the machine as if dangling from the talons of a demon over the fires of hell. Part of me thought about panic, but the peyote fused my mind with the rushing air, the blurry landscape, and the sheer speed of the machine. I was the road, the snake of travel. Fear couldn't catch us, not in the twilight, that time where change rules and no form is constant. The sun retreated beyond the western horizon and darkness began its infiltration of the sky. As the light diminished, Rufus increased the speed. I held on to the bike and did my job, a true passenger in the race against the night.

We arrived in darkness, and it seemed a miracle had been performed. Rufus went into the shack, no doubt to fix some junk, while I walked the path to my house, admiring the stars twinkling within a neurochemical firmament.

Things were quiet the next morning. Carrot and Dick had returned in the wee hours and were still asleep. My head echoed with the psychedelic detritus from the day before, a not unpleasant sensation if I limited myself to slow motion. I sat on the back porch and peeled an orange while I inspected the jumble of lizard-patrolled weeds that we called a yard. As I stared at space, I saw someone creeping through the foliage, moving slowly, crouched, as if advancing for the kill. I couldn't figure out who it was or why they were sneaking around, so I stood to get a better view. The figure saw me and straightened briefly, waving me over. It was Tubbs. He crouched behind a bush and waited. Amused, I walked through the weeds.

"You know the barn across the creek?" Tubbs, usually the epitome of calm, looked worried. "Me, Drone, and Smelly are hiding there. We left the boring Hog Farm thing and went on to another party. Then feds raided, late last night. They rounded everybody up. They wanted someone political, I think. Eventually, our guard looked the other way, so we high-tailed it out of there. Damn. Been walking all night. But we've gotta get fucking gone, you know?" I did. The FBI or Narcotics Bureau or whoever it was wouldn't like anyone escaping their grasp. They might find it suspicious, or just insulting. "Call Gil," Tubbs said. "Ask him to get us out of here. And have somebody bring food and water to the barn. Thanks, man."

Tubbs handed over a scrap with Gil's phone number and retreated into the brush. I was sympathetic, but my first thought was what the fuck? I'm supposed to call? It seemed like too much responsibility. I knew nothing about saving the day. However, I happened to be there, and I didn't see any way to slough off the assignment. I'd been designated and they were counting on me. I berated myself for this latest bout of nerves: settle down, just go call Gil; worry later. I went into the house, gathered a few coins, woke Carrot, and asked him to take provisions to the refugees. The only accessible telephone in the village was in a booth next to the post office. Gil lived in Española, thirty miles away, so it'd be a local call, not too expensive. As I walked over to the PO, I wondered if I had the stuff of a real revolutionary.

When I called, Gil answered. I said my name and briefly explained the situation and asked if he could help Tubbs and the others. I finished and listened to a long pause. "Are you a cop?" he asked. I didn't take offense; it seemed like a relevant question.

"No way," I said. Later, when the dust had settled, Gil told this story several times. Each time when he came to the part about asking if I was a cop, he said, "Oh man, the way you said it, I knew you weren't a cop. No way!" I didn't understand how I said it, but I guess my voice carried enough authenticity to satisfy Gil's radar for heat. "Okay then," he'd told me, "have them at mile 10 on the Canjillon road at midnight." The phone went dead.

I took a roundabout way to the barn, checking to make sure I wasn't followed. Vallecitos could have been a village in the mountains of Old Mexico, it was so sleepy. Nothing ever happened. And nobody followed me. I passed on Gil's message to Tubbs and left them in the barn, talking about hiking through the woods to the rendezvous. I didn't see them again for months, not until they'd been to Seattle and back. By that time, their story had filtered back to us and become legend. They had gone to the mile mark on the Canjillon road, a dirt road through the mountains, and waited. Promptly at midnight, a car drove up, driven by one of Gil's friends. He drove them all the way to Denver, feeding them lines of cocaine and cans of Coors. When they got to the bus station, he gave them enough money for tickets to Seattle. I thought it was cool, their escape through the revolutionary underground. A reminder that in a pinch, it's good to have comrades with means.

The refined peyote I brought back from the party didn't last long. Everybody proclaimed it was a stellar high and wanted more. I made inquiries about the woman I'd met at the Hog Farm gathering. No one knew her name, where she went, or whether there was any more of that peyote floating around. I grieved for a while. I listened to endless speculation about how the cactus might be boiled down and whether it was a good idea or if dried buttons were better, and we should experiment the next time we got a fresh batch, if that ever happened. Like so much in the drug culture, the idea evaporated into the mist of rumors and myths. As for me, the thought crossed my mind that the people you meet on the peyote road aren't necessarily real. At least, don't assume you'll see them again.

5

Poached Elk & Tarantula

Few women crossed the threshold of our adobe house in Vallecitos, and when they did, they didn't stay long. You couldn't hold that against them. It was a simple four-room dwelling occupied by three men: Kid Carrot, Dick, and me. We wanted it funky, so we'd furnished it with a spare assortment of borrowed or stolen antiques that gave it the air of a Victorian bordello. We had brass beds and beaded lampshades, but we never cleaned the place. With no incentive to change, we maintained the same domestic style from the houseboat we had shared in Seattle. There, when the dirty dishes filled the sink, we threw them in the trash and went to the Salvation Army for cheap replacements. My mother would have been mortified, knowing that I'd been raised to know better, but she never saw the houseboat or the adobe house, and I had no reason to show her.

Carrot harbored an obsessive fondness for spiders. It didn't take much to get him to expound on arachnid ethology. The subject became a common conversation during inebriated sessions around the kerosene lamp. One day Smelly, after driving back from the liquor store, handed Carrot a brown paper bag. In the bottom of the bag crouched a tarantula he'd noticed crossing the road. It was large enough to spot from a moving car and, according to Smelly, "he barely avoided a head-on collision." Being a thoughtful friend, Smelly had coaxed the spider into the bag that he'd been using to conceal his forty-ounce bottle of malt liquor. Carrot, of course, was in love. "I'm going to call him Dog," he said.

Carrot introduced Dog to the house by gently setting the open bag on the floor and tipping it on its side. Dog promptly scurried under the couch and disappeared. Carrot fretted, but the rest of us forgot about the spider. A week later, we sat in the living room watching acid patterns on the plaster when Carrot calmly noted that the spider was strolling across the middle of the floor. None of us moved a muscle, rapt in study. If you were in the right frame of mind, you could appreciate the creature's fierce beauty. Dog was a brown desert tarantula about five inches across, and every feature was covered in ghastly hair. If a nightmare could take shape, surely this was it. Yet it moved with stately grace across the linoleum, heading for the corner. When it got there, it used its front legs to slowly climb and prop itself against the two walls, parked at about 45 degrees. It didn't shift this posture, not for a long time.

We stared at the beast, at first with excitement that it was doing something, then with the enhanced focus of psychedelic determination. Hours might have passed in this tableau. We didn't have anything else to do, and nobody was going to bed anytime soon. Instead, we communed with our spider brother, or sister, whichever.

In the wee hours, a beetle appeared, crawling across the floor on some inscrutable coleopteran mission. Staying near the wall, it ventured past the spider. With blistering speed, the tarantula pounced, landed on top of the beetle, and devoured it. The procedure took only an instant. "Jesus Christ!" I said, a sentiment echoed by the others. We didn't know whether to worship or fear. Or both. Meal over, the spider returned to the corner and resumed its ambush.

I didn't sleep well after that. My brass bed, with polished metal legs, seemed to present an unlikely ascent for the chunky little tarantula. Still, the thought lodged in my head that I might wake to find it marching over my face looking for beetles or fleas. Carrot patiently explained that it was nearly impossible for the spider to bite a human, their teeth or fangs or whatever weren't at the right angle and they wouldn't want to, you know, really quite shy, and if they did, their venom was mild, like a bee sting, and on and on he lectured with a pedantic array of natural history lore, none of which helped in the least. When Smelly came by, he would let the spider crawl up and down his arm, a spectacle I observed once, more than enough. In theory, I wanted to find the creature fascinating; in reality, it terrified me.

Our fridge and cupboards were usually bare. When the monthly allotment of food stamps came in, we splurged at the market, but it never lasted long. I'm not saying we spent it wisely; we just spent it. Whatever cash income we had was derived from the black market, which meant we were unemployed in the eyes of the state, and thus eligible for welfare. We exploited this system without shame; everybody signed up and we eagerly collected our food stamps from the post office. Eventually, the New Mexico Human Services Department sent a case worker out for a home visit.

It was a surprise, but we were home, like always. The state lady, a middle-aged Latina, appeared at the door, beaming wholesome cheer, and asked if she could come in and interview everyone. Mrs. Hernandez, she was, and her perfume reminded me of my mother. Rather than putting her on the ratty couch, we supplied her with a kitchen chair while we lined up on the well-worn cushions. She started with neutral demographic queries, then eased into the touchier questions about work histories, income, and other potentially incriminating data. She sat primly, neatly dressed in a dull-colored skirt and blouse, a neutral figure, jotting down her notes amidst the bohemian squalor of our home. We might have looked outlandish to her, skinny young Anglo men with abundant hair, improperly washed, slouching in well-worn clothes. Being a veteran of her profession, she didn't bat an eye.

After fifteen minutes of interview, the tarantula strolled out from under the couch, perhaps curious about the new scent. Mrs. Hernandez spotted it right away and her jaw dropped open. "There... there's a... tarantula!" She pointed with the sharp end of her ballpoint.

We also saw the tarantula, a rare daytime emergence. Carrot waved his hand dismissively and with a bored tone stated, "Oh, that's just Dog."

Outrage, astonishment, fear, and disgust flickered across the face of Mrs. Hernandez in a competitive array. None of these reactions settled into command of her features. Instead of deciding what to say, she hastily bundled up her papers and headed for the door. Over her shoulder, as she crossed the threshold, she said, "We'll finish later."

But we never did. And the food stamps arrived in the mail every month.

Perhaps inspired by the tarantula's hunting successes, Dick raved about trying for some real game, but he never brought anything home. He claimed that we could easily supplement our tedious nutrients with nature's bounty. We nodded eagerly, although none of us hunted and nothing seemed easy about it. Dick went out, though, with his rifle, and combed the woods. He desperately wanted an elk, which certainly carried a lot of meat, but it was the majestic rack of antlers that drove him on. A trophy to mount and stick on a wall, somewhere? His ambitions never seemed clear to me.

One fall afternoon, after being out most of the day, Dick bounced his pickup into the driveway, braking to an abrupt, dusty halt. "Got an elk!" he said. He'd already driven back to recruit Smelly and White for helping him drag the carcass to the truck. Now he'd brought it home. Dick beamed with the pride of his deed while we stood around the open tailgate and stared at the deceased animal. I tried to imagine how it must have looked grazing in the forest, but it was too dead. Four points on each antler; not massive, but still a big rack. Grunting and swearing, we slid it off the truck and onto a tarp, which we then carried around to the rear of the house. Dick would have to butcher it; nobody else had any idea what to do.

He labored into the night, carving the body into a variety of chunks and slabs. The first few steaks went straight into a pan to cook while we transferred the meat to the refrigerator. It was a lot of meat, maybe a couple hundred pounds. By the time we finished, every inch of space in the fridge contained stacked packages of elk. Dick bragged about how he was going to give away some to everybody he knew. The next several days, he drove around and delivered meat like Meals On Wheels, each time retelling the story of his exploits to the admiring recipients.

The antlers confounded him, though. Having grown out of the skull, they couldn't be sliced off with a sharp knife. Stymied, Dick left the beast's head on the back porch, along with the skin, which he said he would tan. The next time Smelly and White walked down from the other house, they saw the elk head. "Get rid of it," White said. "That's not cool."

White was only talking sense. After all, it wasn't hunting season for elk, nor did Dick have a New Mexico hunting license. He dismissed these concerns as straight world bullshit and irrelevant to those of us living outside the law. Smelly pointed out that we'd all be in jeopardy and Dick reluctantly agreed to take care of it. But he wanted those antlers and needed time to figure out how to extricate them from the surrounding bone. We didn't press him, just noticed that the head and the hide disappeared from the back porch. We forgot about it, content to eat steaks twice a day, a welcome addition to our usual diet of beans and chili peppers.

The daily menu of wild meat soon grew tedious. I found myself chewing on steak after steak with diminishing enthusiasm. Nobody knew how to cook stews, roasts, or other variations; it was steak with beans, steak with eggs, steak with potatoes.

However exotic the taste at first, it eventually seemed no different than gnawing on your tongue.

Our tedium was relieved when we returned home one afternoon to find several officers from the New Mexico Department of Game & Fish standing on the porch. The elk head sat on the ground next to one of their trucks. They said they wanted a look at our fridge. Dick shuffled around, kicking at the dirt, while the cops searched the house, emptying the refrigerator, packet after packet. Carrot and I stared at Dick, needling him with our best "what the fuck" expressions. Officer Smith, the Anglo in charge, wanted to know if there was any meat in any other refrigerators around the state. Dick, nervous, ratted everybody out. Officer Smith thanked him for his cooperation; he also thought to ask Dick why he'd been so careless with the remnants of the animal. It turned out that Dick's version of concealing the evidence meant throwing the head into the bushes behind the outhouse where it was eventually spotted by one of the villagers.

While we meditated on Dick's stupidity, we were handcuffed and tucked into the back of a state car, all three of us. The other game officials drove off to corral the rest of the meat and its keepers. Carrot and I glared at Dick, who had fed us for two weeks and was now on the shit list.

It being late Sunday afternoon, the courthouse was closed, so Officer Smith drove us directly to the home of the presiding judge. To facilitate after-hours justice, the judge maintained an office attached to his garage. When we parked in his driveway, the judge was getting out of a car with his wife and children. Smith informed us that they'd been on the verge of going out to Sunday dinner when he'd been radioed about the case and had returned home. We stood in his driveway, handcuffed, and watched the family, in their Sunday finest, troop back into the house. The judge led us around to the side and unlocked a door. We followed him into a room furnished with little more than a long wooden desk, a state flag, an American flag, and a row of chairs facing the desk. Handcuffs were removed and we were waved to the seats. At the front of the desk, the judge placed a black nameplate engraved with white letters: The Honorable E. Maestes. He sat in a well-padded office chair, tapped the desk with a gavel, and declared, "Court's in session."

Officer Smith spoke highly of us as he gave his embarrassing report. "They've been real cooperative, Your Honor."

Judge Maestes asked each of us if we denied the charge: possession of illegal elk meat. None of us had the gall to deny it. The judge, surely thinking about his family and the dinner that waited, pronounced judgment. A fine of $300 apiece. Bang went the gavel. "Court is adjourned."

None of us had the cash, as it turned out, so we were handcuffed again, led out of the room and back to the car, where we were taken to jail until we could pay our fines. The going rate for incarceration was five dollars a day. I did the math: two months in the Española jail. I didn't have that kind of money and assumed that I'd have to do the time. We talked about it; nobody wanted to spend three hundred bucks on the goddam elk; we'd have to gut it out. How bad could it be?

I'd been in a few jails by this time and considered myself something of a hardened criminal. A delusion, of course; I wasn't hard at all, but grandiose, sometimes. The Española jail looked like something left over from the set of a Western movie. Beyond the booking desk was a barred gate and beyond that a dim hallway. About half a dozen cells were accessible to the hall, which ended in a caged day room. The day room contained two metal tables with attached benches. Everything was gray and dingy, bare concrete and steel. Even the toilets were metal. A couple of bored Latinos lounged at one table in the day room, smoking cigarettes. As soon as we were locked in, the guards brought dinner. It turned out that all meals were the same: a shallow bowl of pinto beans in gruel plus a flour tortilla. The beans were cooked with green chilis so hot that the resulting substance should have been labeled radioactive. I prided myself on my taste for chilis and had won several barroom chili-eating contests with my friends, but these beans proved to be too much. We ate what we could and gulped down plastic cups of Kool-Aid.

As soon as we finished, the guards commenced the evening routine. In groups of two, we were ushered out of the day room and along the hall to the last cell. Inside were stacks of thin, well-used mattresses. We each hoisted one and were directed back down the hall. We entered an empty cell, and the guard locked the door. The cell contained four bunks and a toilet. I took a bottom bunk while Carrot grabbed the other. That left Dick upstairs. Blankets or sheets were not provided. We sat glumly, contemplating how one might endure two months in a hellhole.

Soon, the guards came in with three more prisoners. Smelly and White were put in the cell next to ours, while we received the other guy, Stan. He was a scientist at the Los Alamos National Laboratory, where he worked doing secret research for the government. He had the misfortune to be an old high school friend of Dick's and had received a large gift of meat several days ago, followed by today's visit from the game officers once Dick had squealed. For some reason, Stan didn't seem upset with Dick; maybe he knew him too well. Stan was hyper and talked in spurts of pressured mania, thrilled because it was his first experience in jail. At first, he was entertaining, but his inability to slow down and shut up interfered with my ability to find the detached, sluggish trance necessary for doing two months of time.

When they'd rounded up the other three, the judge was unavailable, already occupying his restaurant seats, no doubt, so they'd been brought straight to jail and would be arraigned the next morning.

Stan kept us up late with his jabber, and when the guards woke us at six, we were sore. They made us haul our mattresses back to the storage cell where they were locked up for the day. We trooped to the day room and had breakfast: more beans and Kool-Aid. At that point, we had a choice: either hang out in the day room until lunch or go back to the cell. Carrot and I chose the cell, a mistake. Without the mattresses, we were forced to sit directly on the bunks, which consisted of interlaced steel bands and nothing else. Not just uncomfortable, the steel dug into your flesh and proved to be painful. It was hard to understand why we couldn't have the mattresses, but that was the routine. If they wanted to encourage everybody to gather in the day room, it certainly worked.

After our three friends were led away to court, they didn't return. Stan had money and paid his fine as soon as he saw the judge. He also paid for Smelly and White in a burst of solidarity that didn't extend to the rest of us. Thinking about the implications after we heard this news, Dick suddenly remembered that he had a bank account and when he got the guard's attention, he went out, made a phone call, and was soon released. Carrot and I were left to stew with the volcanic chili.

A couple of days went by. Every day was the same. Up at six, lock up the mattress, spend the day in the common room, don't talk with the Latinos because they didn't want to fraternize with Anglo hippies, go hungry since it was impossible to eat a full bowl of lava, talk until there was nothing more to talk about, run through the incarceration math, curse Dick, and feel the increments of despair entombed in the nature of every prison.

On the fifth day, Carrot decided he'd call in a favor. Before the sun set, he was gone. I faced fifty-five more days of my sentence. With no one else for company, the Latinos took pity on me and gave me cigarettes and sympathy. They still kept mostly to themselves, talking Spanish and adopting postures of practiced cool. It seemed clear to me that I'd lose my mind if I had to spend two months in this jail. I vacuumed up all my pride and asked to make a phone call. I called my parents. Of course, they didn't want their son languishing in a rathole jail in New Mexico, no matter how much I might have deserved it. They agreed to wire the money right away.

The guards also had a routine procedure for this operation. Western Union notified the jail as soon as the wire arrived. Escorted by a single guard, I was released from the cell and driven to the Western Union office to collect the money order. Back at the jail, I received instructions on signing the money over.

"To the State of New Mexico?" I asked.

"No, no, to Judge Enrique Maestes, *si*."

I could have been surprised, but I wasn't. Whatever, it worked. My wallet and jacket were returned to me, and I walked out into the sunlight, free again. Until the next time, it was starting to seem like a habit. I walked over to the highway so I could hitchhike back to Vallecitos. I hoped whoever picked me up had some weed and didn't stop for tarantulas.

6

Shadow Freight

Only a fool tries to get on or off a moving freight train. The floor of a boxcar overhangs the ground by almost five feet, higher if the tracks are on a berm, and getting in requires athletic determination. If you falter, your legs tend to swing under the car. When the car is moving, you could end up on the rail, amputated. Caution is also required for the dismount: I watched an impatient friend of mine leap from a slow-rolling train. He was lucky; he only broke his arm. I saw that and stayed on board, leaving him behind. In time, the train would stop; they always do. I learned these things when I rode the rails off and on for three years, starting at age nineteen. I knew the feds were after me for draft evasion, so I wandered from place to place, never staying anywhere more than a month or a week or however long it took to wear out my welcome. Then I'd stuff my belongings in a rucksack and hike to the freight yard. That was my freedom.

They say young men test themselves against the darkness for initiation, a rite of passage into adulthood. I didn't find any rituals, just a lot of darkness. But then, I wasn't exactly an initiate; I was a bum. For stability, I clung to my derelict associates. We were a restless, dissipated lot, moving about the American West with an urgency that belied our cool demeanor. And freight trains were the way to travel, I was told, unless you wanted to hitchhike, subjecting yourself to roadside abandonments or encounters with highway predators. We'd all had our share of that, so in the winter of 69 when we decided to travel from northern New Mexico to Mardi Gras in New Orleans, we chose to go as freight.

Entering the Albuquerque freight yard for the first time, I felt like a mouse on the freeway. Everything was metal-hard, noisy, huge, and stank of diesel. I'd seen nothing like it: endless ranks of freightcars, boxcars, all sorts of cars, each one emblazoned with an icon of origin. They read like grail beacons, clues to divergent directions: Great Northern, Santa Fe, Reading, Erie Lackawanna, Delaware & Hudson, Seaboard, Rock Island, Union Pacific; the world, it seemed, passed through a roundhouse. My head spun with the promises. When I saw four linked and sooty engines flowing down a track, rumbling with power, ready to drag away one of those chains, I felt a yearning I'd never acknowledged. This was the way, the path, the coupling for my shadow.

We got off to a breezy start, five of us blowing a little weed, hyped up on beatnik traditions and confident of a Good Time. The boxcar was new, a cushion ride (advertised in giant letters on the side) and I slept the whole way south to El Paso, lulled to a rocking sleep, snuggled by a warm carnival dream. In the black night of the El Paso yard, they started breaking down the train into segments for other destinations. We climbed off our smooth ride, and searched for an eastbound, not easy in the unlabeled maze of switching freight. In the darkness and confusion, I fell behind and lost sight of the others. Maybe I dawdled or got distracted, but it felt like I'd passed into a private world. I was alone, and afraid. Trapped between lines of cars, I panicked and didn't know which way to go. Crossing from one track to another required clambering over the couplings between cars, a dangerous feat, because the lines shifted without warning, shoved by an engine sometimes a quarter mile away. The couplings were loose, like interlocking knuckles, allowing the train to stretch or contract as it moved. When cars were slammed together, the sound was explosive; if you were nearby, you flinched. Easy to imagine what it might be like to be caught between metal and metal. You'd be maimed or dead, another wasted transient. I scrambled over the couplings anyway and stepped up my pace in the alleys, nerves taut, searching for my friends, an eastbound train, anything that offered a solution to the steel puzzle of the yards.

    I trudged in a stupor back and forth through the yard. Without a watch, I had no sense of time; it seemed bottomless. I walked on the ties of an empty track for a while, an automaton lost in the night, until I sensed something different, a shift of air, perhaps. I didn't bother to turn, I just threw myself to the side, barely dodging a boxcar rolling up behind me, a silent peril. Gasping, I sprawled in the rocks and watched the gloom reclaim the car as it slid toward its assignment. The smell of oil and diesel filled my lungs. How did I end up like this, curled on the ground, utterly pathetic? My eyes watered, but I refused to cry. My heart pounded on, marching through my eardrums; a pulse broken by the distant chugging of yard engines shuffling rows of cars. Now what? I didn't know what to do. Sure, I'd nearly been killed, but it was so impersonal, so random, it meant nothing. Regardless, I couldn't keep staggering around without a plan. I hiked away from the tracks, crawled into the bushes at the perimeter of the yard and retreated into my sleeping bag.

With the early sun, reason returned, and the anxieties of the night became a dull memory. I cooked Roman Meal over canned heat. I didn't want to think about being crazy or nearly getting crushed. Better to consign it to the underworld where nightmares belong. Walking back into the yard, I ran into another bum who told me I'd missed three eastbound trains during the night. Clearly, I needed to get my shit together. Poking around the yards, I found one of my friends, my old buddy Carrot. He, too, had been lost in his own version of the iron dream. The others? Gone, it seemed, on an eastbound sailing all the way to New Orleans. Carrot could have gone with them, but hung back, looking for me. So now we were together, the remnants.

My experiences in the yard left me rattled, but the intensity had hit me like a drug. Steel was dangerous, yet we were alive, tempered by the exposure to an unyielding reality. We couldn't give up; our friends would snicker and drown us with tales of what we'd missed. Time to knuckle down. We roamed the yards, trying to decipher the anonymous rows of cars, trying to find the key to getting out. Desperate, we asked a switchman about the eastbound. He took pity on us, or maybe he was always kind to bums. We followed him across several tracks to a line of cars hitched to three engines, rumbling and straining, ready to go. He pointed to an open boxcar. "Have a good ride," he said.

It was late afternoon when we chugged out of El Paso. Both doors of the boxcar were wide open, so we sat towards the front, out of the wind, and stared at the passing desolation of Texas. We wolfed our rations of bread and sardines, washing it down with slugs from a pint of cheap tokay. I'd started drinking tokay after I ran into a street bum who chanted, over and over, "Tokay is okay!" I figured that guy had an inside track on the road to oblivion, so I decided that I, too, should drink tokay. I couldn't duplicate his enthusiasm, though, because it tasted like grape juice mixed with kerosene. But it had a kick; that was the point.

It was a rough ride through plains of sagebrush, a winter landscape that embodied the bleak. Time passed without meaning as the train hurtled down the line. If the boxcar ever had shock absorbers, they would be exhausted from years of hauling freight. We quickly gave up trying to stretch out and relax; every turn of the wheels bounced us up and down, a bruising, body-slamming ordeal. We sat on our packs, propped against the wall of the car, and stared out at the scrubland, always the same, hour after hour, unrelieved by trees or water or signs of animal life. Every now and then the train would slow down, for no reason that we could tell, but whenever it did, we stretched out and hoped for a nap or just a respite.

The train didn't stop for a day and a half, rumbling on through periods of speed and sloth, driving us to an edgy exhaustion. Nothing we could do about it. Once on, there's no way to get off until it stops. In the middle of the night, the train slowed to a crawl, passing through new yards. They were huge, clearly part of a city, another maze. Where were we? The train stopped.

But where? It's hell not knowing where you are. And freight yards don't provide signposts.

We heard the crunch of gravel underfoot. A yard bull, the railroad police. "Awl-right boys, GIT OFF!" He drawled it, Texas-style. I asked where we were. "San Antonio. Now git outta here fast!" I could tell he was no bullshit, but my legs were shot from riding the train, knees turned to jello; scrambling off the car I fell on my face in the rocks. Before the bull could pick me up, I jumped to my feet and tore off after Carrot. We made a beeline for the edge of the yards and escaped into the city. Most yard workers don't care about bums, but the railroad police are a different matter. On some lines they look the other way, on some they hunt you down. We had no desire to test this guy, he sounded mean as hell. Or maybe it was just the accent.

The road to New Orleans divided us in San Antonio. We split up for better luck with hitchhiking; there didn't seem to be any other option. I said goodbye to Carrot and surrendered to the fools of the highway. I got a ride alright, but it turned into a disaster; I barely escaped with my life. That soured me on hitchhiking, but freight trains, no, they would be fine.

A month or two later, back in Seattle, I hung around with friends, got high, scammed and schemed, but did nothing of substance, mostly just wasted time. It didn't take long to regain the itch, the urge for movement. Staying in one place brought up too many questions. I told myself I had to stay ahead of the Draft Board, but I would have been running even without that excuse. I couldn't stay put, even in the city, and walked the streets at night, alone. At some point I would pack a bag and leave, going south or maybe east, somewhere else. The point was in the going.

It was early spring when I found myself in Spokane's Northern Pacific yards looking for a westbound back to Seattle. Hours went by without a train. I walked around the yards to stay warm and asked all the workers about the westbound, but the answer was the same shrug and a maybe. The sun went down so I retired to the hobo camp at the edge of the yard. I had a pint of cheap whiskey; I drank it while I sat on my pack. I wondered when the fucking NP line was going to send a goddamn train. I heard myself say it out loud. Or mutter, really, snarling through my beard like the other burnt-out bums. Why not; wasn't that who I was? It's the bottle that kept despair at bay; that's why you have to keep drinking.

Another bum came by. We talked, but like many railroad veterans, his speech was hard to understand. Even when I could make out the words, the sentences didn't add up to much more than a jumble. His interior must have been the same, I figured. The railroad experience can shake your hold on language. It scared me, listening to his babble. We gave up our attempts at dialogue and sat side by side, finishing the whiskey, separated by the mute boundaries of our private realms.

Dawn came and with it a westbound freight, so I was off again. A short train pulled by powerful engines, it jerked and bounced so hard that once again I couldn't lay down and had to brace myself against the boxcar wall. The pounding dulled my wits, and I gazed vacantly out the open door at the blur of wheatfields and sagebrush.

Eventually, the train lost speed and rolled into a yard at a walking pace. I scanned the surrounding city while my nerves decelerated. It was my hometown, the arid flatland where I grew up. I thought about calling my folks but settled for climbing on a new freight, Seattle-bound. I couldn't find an empty boxcar, just a grain car, a sealed trapezoid-shaped container with a small open platform tucked at each end. There's just enough room on either side of the coupling to sit scrunched up, pack tucked under your knees. I'd never ridden a grain car, but there didn't seem to be a choice if I wanted to ride.

As I scrambled aboard, a man sitting at the adjacent corner of the grain car raised a hand in greeting. He said he was a migrant worker heading for the cherry orchards. He looked and talked like Woody Guthrie, a man of experience, so I figured if he could ride there, I could, too. But when he started talking about a bad-ass brakeman down the line that'd take your roll or throw you in jail, I smiled and paid it no mind. You hear that crap everywhere, classic hobo lore, something to impress the novices.

We talked amiably but had to stop when the train rolled out. The driver poured on the speed. I sat on the steel platform a few feet above the tracks, and the pounding was intense, even worse than the last ride. The other fellow grimaced like he wasn't enjoying it either. The train seemed to get faster with every mile, and we hurtled along in a bruising frenzy. My eyes were riveted on the wheels of the car behind us, and I watched how they slid back and forth against the rails looking to jump the tracks at any time. When I glanced at the migrant, his eyes were big and I knew he had the same thought: in a derailment, we'd be crushed beyond recognition, laid to rest in a sealed box. Fear tightened every muscle until I thought I'd explode—then a safety valve gave way and I didn't care. I placed myself in the grave and threw the first shovel of dirt, who gives a shit.

The train kept rolling and paid no mind to us. It stopped briefly in Yakima, the migrant jumped off, and I rode on through the mountains into Auburn, the NP freight yard just south of Seattle. The long walk into the city gave me a chance to clear my head. Then it was back to crashing at the houses of friends, acquaintances, or whoever would put up with me. Hanging around the streets was like coming home: "Hey, where ya been?" Getting in on drug deals just to get a little cut, eating what I could scrounge, living close to the bone, that was my life. By then, riding freights was a constant. Anytime I wanted to go somewhere or get out of town, I'd head to the yards. I hardened to the ordeal and even welcomed it as a masochistic rite, a kind of gravity for my restless soul.

Heading north or east, I rode out of Seattle's Great Northern yard. Bums favored it because the GN had a reputation for tolerance to stowaways. You could hang around the yard forever, asking questions, and no one would chase you away. From there it was simple to catch a ride to Bellingham, a short hop of eighty miles, and I made that trip many times. Especially if I needed new places to crash. Without friends scattered around the West, I don't know how I would have managed. One time, I set up on a northbound boxcar, jug of water, beef jerky, slabs of cardboard to cushion my butt, just leaning back against the wall blowing a few reefers and watching the coast roll by through the open door, better than a picture window. The tracks followed the shore with the waters of Puget Sound lapping the rocks below the railroad ties. Content, I watched the sun flash across the swelling surface, almost audible with golden tones. The run went slow and easy and two hours later we pulled into Bellingham. I might have been restless in a counterproductive way, but sometimes the movement provided a pleasure of freedom I didn't know how to get otherwise.

Summer always brought the itch to escape. I blamed the city, of course. The rain wouldn't let up, and as the air warmed, so did the odors of decay. Time to move, stay ahead of the rot, so one morning, I crawled on an eastbound Great Northern and left Seattle. All the boxcars had been sealed shut, forcing me onto another grain car. As usual, the car was a tough ride, especially in the eight-mile-long Cascade tunnel under Stevens Pass, handkerchief to nose all the way, choking on diesel fumes and buried in absolute blackness. If underworld mythology took an industrial detour, it would go through here. Finally, after the eerie passage through the dark, we left the tunnel, bursting into the clean, hard sunshine of Eastern Washington.

I changed trains in Spokane, lucky to get a hot shot to Chicago. I only found one empty boxcar and it already had guys in it. I preferred to ride alone, it was safer that way, but if I wanted the fast freight, I'd have to share. What the hell; I climbed on. The first guy I noticed was a giant Native man with the color and countenance of red granite. He nodded at me. The other three riders, all White, sat or stood or paced around the car. A restless, frizzy-haired man seemed like a veteran hobo; his clothes were rags and he babbled psychotic word salad in a steady monologue. A teenager sat cross-legged on a piece of cardboard, clutching a .22 rifle. When I looked at him, he announced that he'd run away from home. Maybe the gun made him feel safer. The last guy was the weirdest: a middle-aged, well-groomed man wearing a tidy business suit and leaning against the boxcar wall like it was a file cabinet in his office. Everybody was drunk. The party had started, and it picked up the pace when we pulled out of the yards. I was curious about my companions, but you'd never get the truth out of them. We all knew that and settled for sharing a fifth of tokay, telling lies as we rolled through the wilds of northern Idaho and Montana, savoring the fair weather and the shitty wine.

Every now and then we passed a ghost town, wooden relics harboring dreams of the frontier gone to seed. I studied these remnants, fascinated with the traces of human ambition reclaimed by the wild country. I looked at the land the way I looked in the mirror, looking for something. But the train wasn't a quest. No tarnished grail lay buried in railroad earth waiting for a hobo to recognize its value and wipe off the grime. The frontier wasn't a hero's treasure, it was a state of mind, a flight from the known, propelled by the fear of reckoning.

In the middle of the night, I slipped out of the boxcar, train dead still in Havre, Montana. Without a parting word I left behind a group of people with whom I'd shared a bottle or two but didn't trust. Yet their companionship had eased my mind, distracted me, and I missed them anyway. The road before me was long and lonely, a giant stretch all the way to New Mexico. Nervous with movement, feeling that strung-out thinness of fiber, I yearned for an end, a bed to rest, a woman to share it.

Early in the morning, I got a CB&Q flatcar to Denver. My ride was stacked with lumber, and I crawled on top of the load, open to the sky, and hoped for good weather. There was another bum on the train; I saw him when I walked the line of cars. I asked him a question and watched him try to say something, but the poor bastard could only gurgle and croak, he was so wracked out.

The train rode smoothly through a fantasy landscape: the Wyoming backcountry and its big sky horizon, no towns, no roads, just a high desert range populated by enormous herds of antelope. They moved with freedom and grace; it made me envious. I told myself that I rode the freights to get from one place to another, to avoid the law, but that wasn't it. I rode the freights to be on the freights, a realm apart. Once I'd thought that I might do things, write a book or two, but here I was, a lonely tramp rolling over the land, a shadow on the back of an industrial snake, lost in reflection and raw with the pain that doesn't speak. I could see it now: riding solo on the freights was too powerful an experience: you had to be drunk or crazy. I'd carried my home in a pack for so long that I couldn't relate to a permanent roof as anything other than a pit-stop. Talk about lost. I needed to get off. Off, before I became that bum back there, strangling in the effort to find words.

The train chugged into Denver and stopped; I'd have to find a new one to go further south. The delay felt unbearable, but I sat in the yards and waited for a southbound (always waiting for a –bound, like Jelly Roll Morton says, "If you was going someplace, that's where you was bound…"). Maybe I would stay in New Mexico this time. It was a place; there were friends and community. Maybe I could put things to rest.

It was a sunny day in Colorado, and I let the warmth stoke a little optimism in my heart. A yard worker came up to me and I told him I was looking for the southbound. He grinned and darted his eyes around and shoved a dollar in my hand and I smiled thanks even though I had fifty more in my pocket.

The worker's kindness stayed with me even after heading out on one more infernal grain car. His gesture seemed incredible, an act of faith. I tried to think above the rumble of the train. One thing seemed obvious. If I stayed the course, sooner or later I'd arrive at oblivion. I'd been able to keep the feds and the draft behind me. That had been my reason for running, or so I told myself, but the painful emptiness of my life couldn't be escaped. At heart, I wasn't as enamored of nothingness as I'd boasted. I didn't know what I was looking for, or what I wanted, but crossing the final threshold was not it. This had to be the last ride, the end of wallowing in diesel soot and pretending that the grime gave me cover, a disguise.

7

The Subject

When I was twenty years old, like a child, I followed my friends and did what they did. I don't think any of us had much self-awareness. Instead, we moved in packs and adopted disguises. Mine was a work in progress as I sampled various themes. For the Mardi Gras trip in the winter of 69 my costume included antique suspenders over a flannel shirt, a button-down tweed cap, work boots, faded jeans, and a worn-thin leather blazer from the 40s that my father had given me to show that he had been cool, once upon a time. Long, greasy hair and a wispy beard completed the look. I carried a battered suitcase crammed with tee shirts, books, underwear, socks, maybe an extra pair of pants. The goal was to look like a dust bowl refugee, god knows why.

When the yard bull kicked us off the train in San Antonio, I ran with the suitcase but stumbled over my awkward thrift store boots. Fear got me back on my feet and kept me going. I raced to catch up with Carrot and we only stopped for breath outside the yards. It was 3 AM, pitch dark, there was no traffic on the street, pedestrian or automotive. Clearly, we'd have to hitchhike to New Orleans, but getting through the sprawl to the correct highway was going to require a lot of walking. We couldn't afford to buy a map, even if we found someplace that sold them. With nothing better to do, we started hiking down the street toward the strongest glow of lights, figuring that's where we'd find the city center, as good a place to start as any.

After about half a mile, a police cruiser pulled alongside. The cop rolled down the passenger window. "Boys," he drawled, "do you know where you are?" I looked at him blankly while Carrot blurted out some nonsense about San Antonio, getting off the train, looking for the highway, and assuring him that we were "Just passing through." The cop nodded, confirming his supposition that we didn't know. "Boys, you're in Darktown. You sure as hell ain't safe here. Get in. I'll take you down the road a piece." If we had needed a crash introduction to the rules of the South, we couldn't have asked for more clarity. We were "boys," but because we were White, we sure didn't belong in "Darktown."

The cop, having saved a couple of White souls, let us sit in his car and drink coffee, then he dropped us near an access ramp to Interstate 10, the eastbound highway out of San Antonio. Despite this good deed, our spirits were low. We had hoped to arrive in New Orleans via private boxcar, delivered like hobo royalty. Instead, we faced the asphalt reality of begging for rides. And what kind of a Texas fool would pick up two grubby hippies, anyway? Hitching together made it harder, so we split up again, diminishing our number to a less threatening proportion. I swallowed my foreboding, shook hands with Carrot, and marched off to the next interstate ramp, calling over my shoulder, "See you in N'awlins!"

Perched on the suitcase, I watched the sun rise as my thumb sagged. I hated hitch-hiking; it was random, unpredictable, and dangerous. One time, I was stuck for three days at the same ramp in Los Angeles, spending the nights rolled up against a fence in the bushes. And when you do get a ride, you always have to deal with the driver. Is he stable, intoxicated, creepy? You must decide quickly. I've had a driver suddenly pull off the road to a secluded spot "for just a minute," and, hand on my thigh, ask, "Do you have a lot of hair down there?" I didn't know what to say. I got out of the car instead and he drove away, leaving me to walk back to the highway. More than one friend advised that the best way to deal with gay cruisers is to "Beat the shit out of 'em and take their roll," but I didn't know how to beat the shit out of anyone, nor did I have the desire. None of those guys ever tried to force it on me, anyway; they'd just get sullen and drive off. Women, of course, have a whole different range of experiences.

I waited for a few hours in San Antonio before a car pulled over, an ill-muffled Chrysler Imperial. There were three in the front, young folks. The passenger door creaked open, and the driver beckoned me into the front while one of the three, a woman, crawled over the seat into the back. I slid into the shotgun position as a long-haired Latino scooted to the middle. The driver was a White guy named Carl, the guy next to me was Jésus, and the woman consigned to the back introduced herself as Wanda. When I told them that I was headed to Mardi Gras in New Orleans, Carl was enthusiastic. "Oh yeah! We'll take you there, man!" I couldn't believe my luck.

But Carl drove fast, too fast. His preference for speed and passing every vehicle on the road terrified me. It hadn't even been a year since the last time I felt this vulnerable on the road. When Carl noticed my hands braced against the dashboard, he tried to reassure me. "Don't worry, man, I'm a truck driver; I do this all the time!" Jésus seemed unperturbed by Carl's driving or, apparently, anything else. He smiled and nodded a lot. Wanda bounced around the back seat, singing and chatting in party mode. I choked down my anxiety and decided to trust Carl. His maneuvers were daring, but he did execute them with skill. Besides, my first ride was a jackpot—all the way to New Orleans! If I remembered nothing else my mother said, I certainly remembered her favorite maxim: "Beggars can't be choosers."

We stopped in Houston at the home of Carl's sister, where he hit her up for money. We waited in the car. Then we drove to the market and bought three cases of beer and several pints of hard stuff before returning to the interstate.

Things got fuzzy after that. I remember we wanted a pit stop to drain the beer and Carl didn't quite make the exit. The car fishtailed around the curve of the ramp, and we flew off the road and landed in spongy grass. While the three of us pushed and heaved, Carl gunned it back to the pavement, leaving tracks gouged across the turf. This could have been a warning, but in accepting Carl's invincibility as a driver, I once again abandoned my agency. I was just a rider.

We crossed the Louisiana border in the dark. We'd consumed all the beer and liquor and lapsed into silence, watching the roadside blur past the headlights. When I glanced at the speedometer, it read 85, but I was drunk and didn't care. Then Carl drifted to the left and the Chrysler slammed into the exposed end of a concrete median. The impact, almost explosive, spun us like a top across the road and onto the shoulder. As soon as we stopped, the engine burst into flames. I saw the fire and had one thought: get out of the car. With my shoulder, I shoved open the door and fell on the road. Using the car door to pull myself to standing, I reached back in for Jésus, who was non-responsive. He might have been alive, still. It's possible that I finished him off by dragging him out of the car. Carl was unconscious and pinned behind the collapsed steering wheel. I looked at Wanda, moaning in the back, but by that time a passing truck driver ran over and took charge of the situation. He had a fire extinguisher. Before long, others arrived, bystanders, state police, and ambulances.

I wandered back and forth in a daze, not knowing what to do. Later, I saw a photo of the wreck. The front of the car was twisted steel. The windshield displayed two impact points with radiating cracks from where Jésus' head and my head crashed into it. Maybe the car had seatbelts, but we wouldn't have worn them, anyway. Wanda ended up with a broken arm from flying around the back. Carl broke his spine, and he was paralyzed from the waist down. Jésus died from internal bleeding. And somehow, I walked. I lost two teeth on the dashboard; other than that, I had nothing to show. I couldn't understand why I was alive.

After the initial chaos at the emergency scene, no one seemed to realize that I had been in the car. There were dozens of people milling around in a confusing tangle of officials and spectators. I watched numbly as my traveling companions were taken away in ambulances. There was still one ambulance at the scene so I walked over to the attendant and asked if I should go to the hospital or what. I tried to explain what happened, but I'm sure between the trauma and the booze I didn't make a lot of sense. Anyway, he told me to sit in the back and we raced off to the emergency room in Baton Rouge.

The ER doc decided that I only had a concussion and there was nothing to be done about the teeth, so he discharged me in less than an hour. It was midnight in Baton Rouge; I had no money and, once again, no idea of what came next. Find a road and keep hitchhiking to New Orleans, I guessed. I didn't see any other choice. As I walked out the door, a nurse ran after me and asked if I would sit and wait for a few minutes. "Just a formality," she said. I returned to the lobby and took a seat.

I waited for a while until a city policeman sauntered up and asked about my plans. When I told him, he said, "Look, how about you come with me. You got no place to stay, so let's put you up for the night. We got some questions to ask, and we can do that in the mornin'. We don't need you out on the streets, okay?"

If I wasn't fatalistic before, by this point I was a complete lamb. Maybe it was the concussion or the drinking or even the learned helplessness that comes from being a bum. Or maybe I remembered the kindness of the police officer on night patrol in San Antonio. Whatever it was, I offered no resistance to the officer's proposal.

The lodging he had in mind was the Baton Rouge City Jail, and that's where he took me. He handed me off to the guards and left. Right away, they ordered me to strip off all my clothes and enter a small, tiled room. After the door shut, pressure jets of insecticide-laden water bombarded every inch of skin. "Just in case you is lousey." After the shower, I stepped out of the tiled room into a circle of half a dozen uniformed men. I stood in the middle, shy and naked. They looked me up and down, nudging each other, sneering and staring through hard, nasty expressions. For the next quarter of an hour or so, I was the subject of a ruthless commentary on my body: its shape, its inadequacies, its questionable sex, and, repeatedly, the likelihood of my anus being penetrated during the night. "Oh yeah, boy, you're gonna get fucked. I guarantee it."

After an eternity of this theater-in-the-round, they allowed me to don prison coveralls and join a couple dozen inmates in a communal cell. I braced for instant assault and rape. A couple of guys stared and one nodded without expression. I figured that if I could get through the night without harm, then the next day, after answering the cop questions, I would get the hell out of Baton Rouge. That was my comfort. Otherwise, I lay awake on the bunk, waiting for the moment when I'd be seized and torn apart, but it never happened. My cellmates were curious, though, like all prisoners. "Whatta you in for?" Beyond that, they could care less.

The next morning, the police didn't ask any questions. Instead, they herded me along with ten or fifteen other prisoners into a large van. There were Black men in the van along with the Whites and we were jammed into suffocating proximity on benches along the wall. Or we sat on the floor between each other's legs.

No one spoke and I didn't dare ask where we were going. I don't think the ride was long but even a few minutes in that sweltering box of unfortunate men felt biblical. In time we arrived, with another van, at the entrance to the Baton Rouge Parish Prison. The guards ordered us to form two lines. It wasn't specified, but one line was Black and the other White. As soon as we started to march into the facility, a Black man fell to the ground. The guards tensed up, pulling their sticks and barking commands. "Keep movin'! Keep movin'!" Someone pointed to the unconscious man and started to ask a question, but the response was a pointed shotgun. "KEEP MOVIN'!" So, the line of Blacks just stepped over the fallen man as if he wasn't there.

When we crossed the portal, the Black line turned one way and the White line turned the other, which was the last time I saw any Blacks in the prison. I shuffled along with the others and we penetrated the depths of the facility via barren gray halls and a succession of barred gates. Prisoners were siphoned from the line to stations along the way. Finally, a door opened, a finger pointed, and I entered my destined cell block. The door slammed with a clang, and I stood in the middle of the common room, perplexed and frightened. This open area, surrounded on three sides by bars so there were no hidden corners, was furnished with fixed metal tables, benches, and about a dozen inmates. A non-stop television droned from the upper corner. The cells, four bunks in each, were down an open hall past the shower and bathroom.

Of course, everyone looks at you as soon as you walk in, gauging your size and posture and any other details that might be useful for influence or survival, depending on whether you were likely to be submissive or dominant. Within minutes, I received a whispered confidence from a weasel-faced character: "Don't drop the soap in the shower, and whatever you do, don't bend over to pick it up." He concluded his advice with a knowing chuckle.

I knew that I was fresh meat. In some situations, that would be enough to start a feeding frenzy like the one I endured from the cops at the city jail. However, in this cell block order was maintained by a short, wiry inmate named Red. He took one look at my hair and delivered judgment. "You're gettin' a haircut." I was dismayed enough to muster a complaint, "Do I have to?" "Boy, I'm not askin'." Red had the tools: clippers, scissors, you name it, and I was quickly shorn. Red had a lot of things that I was surprised to find within a prison, including cutlery. But he was the only one. The guards looked the other way and were generally deferential. After all, he did their job for them. I never saw anyone resist. Red was the boss and that's how it was.

It didn't take long to settle on a strategy: shut up and don't draw attention. Contrary to the scenarios of most prison movies where the quiet guy is used and abused by everyone else in the pecking order, it worked for me. Most of the inmates had better things to do, like play cards for cigarettes. However, one shifty guy, a plump, fast talker, kept taking me aside for subdued conversations. Truthfully, they were monologues. "You want outta this shit hole? I can git you out, yes sir. Three hunnerd, that's all it takes. You get your people to wire it on down. With that, you're home free. I got pull."

The only hitch, aside from the fact that I didn't believe him for a minute, was that I didn't have the money. Perhaps as compensation for the haircut, Red reminded the guards that I was allowed to make a phone call. I dialed my parents collect and told them where I was, trying to ignore the weary resignation in my father's voice. After a few minutes, the guard clicked off the phone, ending my contact with the outside world.

I wasn't charged with a crime, I was never arraigned, no one had asked my name or addressed me in any official process since I left the hospital. I ended up in prison, that's all. Red advised me that I wouldn't get another shot at the phone. You needed privileges for that. I didn't have privileges. I had nothing.

This went on for three weeks. As bad as it was, I got used to it, falling into a numb fog. It was a liminal existence, neither here nor there, a limbo of blank, passing days. Every now and then I'd consider my buddies, wondering if they were having a wild time at Mardi Gras. I didn't think about it much, though, because it seemed like a dangerous luxury to imagine life outside the cellblock.

Aside from pesky attempts to scam, no one bothered me. I read a lot of inane Western novels and whatever other trash was available. Sometimes I watched the television, but it was just as rewarding to stare at the wall. The only real structure revolved around meals, which were surprisingly decent. It was Louisiana, after all, and even prisoners were considered human enough to receive the correct food, so we ate seafood, okra, cornbread, that sort of thing. Sometimes after dinner an inmate would show mercy and give me a cigarette, which I smoked, because in prison, you smoke every chance you get. This provides the apex of the day, and you learn how to smoke so that each single gesture of the act is more complex and meaningful than high mass.

Blending into the cellblock society, I lost track of who I had been before I was a prisoner. Then early one day I heard a guard calling my name through the bars. I hadn't heard it since I'd walked into the jail. I didn't think he meant me, so I sat on the bench like a lump. Red looked at me and angled his head toward the guard; only then did I jump up and go to the cell door.

The guard was terse. "Follow me, boy." We left the compound, walked down some halls, through repetitions of gates, and ended up in a room with two men in suits. For a moment, they studied me without expression. Out came the badges. "Agent Jones, Agent Smith. FBI." Agent Jones stated my name and asked if that's who I was. "Yes," I said, baffled. As always with the FBI, they were efficient. Agent Jones said, "I'm placing you under arrest for failure to report, as ordered, for induction into the United States Army." Agent Smith snapped me in handcuffs.

Almost two years had passed since I failed to report. It was shortly after dropping out of the University of Washington when I received my induction notice. I had taken the notice and my draft card and torn them into tiny pieces and chucked them in the trash. I understood that was a federal crime, but I had no willingness to go to Vietnam and fight that war. If I lived like a bum, with no steady residence, I didn't see how they would locate me. Since then, I'd gone to jail a couple of times for minor offenses and the lack of a draft card hadn't been a problem. At some point, I stopped thinking about it. However, the sharp, suspicious eyes of the Baton Rouge authorities were not fooled. They never said anything to me, of course. They just called the feds.

Other than announcing that I was under arrest, followed by a formal recitation of my rights, Jones and Smith remained mute. Their gestures were economical and polite, smug with the confidence of absolute power over their subject. I wasn't sure whether to be relieved or intimidated but leaned toward the latter as the safest response. It didn't take much to figure out that these guys weren't going to be my new best friends.

Official reunion with my name brought with it the realization that I was now a federal prisoner. As part of this change in status, the agents marched me out of the parish prison. With practiced movements, they herded me into the back seat of a sedan parked in the loading area. When I asked where we were going, Agent Jones gave me one word: "Court."

We drove into the center of Baton Rouge, the second-largest city in Louisiana. The downtown streets were tidy and lined with trees and small parks. Sunshine, the first I'd seen in weeks, warmed the morning air. They parked in a garage and helped me out of the car. Positioning themselves on each side of my body, they were close enough for an immediate takedown, should I decide to flee. Such precautions were unnecessary. They could have rolled me into a dumpster, and I would've stayed there. We walked in formation, Jones to the left, Smith to the right, a classic perp walk. I was handcuffed and still wore prison coveralls. The courthouse was a couple of blocks away, and we strolled through a park and along a busy sidewalk, full of well-dressed bankers and office workers. Everybody made a wide detour around us. I thought I knew what humiliation felt like, but this was a new level. I kept my head down and avoided eye contact and let the agents, hands on my elbows, steer our advance to justice.

We were right on time for the hearing. As they led me into the courtroom, I was amazed to see my father sitting along the aisle. What the hell was he doing here? I had no idea, but just the sight of his concerned, brave face reminded me that I mattered to somebody.

The judge wasted no words. He pointed out that I did not report for induction as duly notified. This was true and I saw no reason to deny it. "Well then, here's what I'm going to do. If you agree to report to the induction center as soon as you are summoned, then I am going to release you into the custody of your father." I quickly agreed. "Alright, then, as he is now your legal custodian, I also order you to do what he says. Am I understood?" Indeed, I understood.

I couldn't believe it. In an antechamber, the agents exchanged the cuffs and coveralls for my old suitcase and clothes, and I walked out of the courthouse with my father.

Over lunch, Dad told his story. After the call from jail, my mother had been frantic. To appease her, he rumbled into action, telephoning people, looking for someone who could clarify the situation and how to deal with it. He hired a private detective who sent newspaper clippings about the wreck (including the grisly photo of the car) and explained to him the peculiarities of Louisiana law. In that state, you can be imprisoned for up to two months without charges. In my case, they threw me in jail and waited for something to surface. Who knows why they bothered? They were clear in their dislike of my long hair. But it could have been anything; why pretend to understand the motivations of law enforcement? Regardless, once my dad understood the circumstances, he booked passage on a train from Spokane, Washington to Baton Rouge.

By 1969, the feds were already tired of draft dodgers clogging the court system, so when my dad met with the prosecutor, it was agreed to drop the charges if I'd just show up for the damn physical. Meanwhile, my father, being an all-American nice guy, had met a Baton Rouge couple who opened their home to him in that warm-hearted way often associated with Southern society. From court, Dad and I went straight to a lunch served around their dining table, an outstanding shrimp gumbo. I felt ashamed of the mess I'd created, but they were hardly fans of "the gummit," and offered sympathy and genuine hospitality. In response to this unearned nurturing, I didn't know what to say, other than a quiet thank you.

The next day we boarded the train north. My dad was proud to have pulled off the rescue and he knew my mother would be pleased, but he wasn't much of a talker, and he had no heart to berate me for my follies. I couldn't bring myself to explain the details of the ordeal and we left it at that. When we talked, we talked of simple things, soothing things. And he never brought it up, not until fifteen years later, when I stopped getting in trouble and finally got around to thanking him for all the help over the years. Then he said, slowly and with the faintest of smiles, "Yeah, that was kind of rough there, wasn't it, down in Louisiana?"

Back home, I returned to my old bedroom, still the way I'd left it, and followed my parents' orders. This was easy because they were issued by my mother and consisted of "finish your potatoes" and things like that. Three weeks later, I received a new draft card in the mail along with a notice to report for induction in Spokane. Since it was scheduled bright and early, the Army paid for a hotel room one block from the induction center, "for your convenience."

I took the bus to Spokane, checked into the room, and walked to the nearest drugstore. Back at the hotel, I locked myself in for the night and focused on slugging down two bottles of Romilar cough syrup, a procedure that took an hour or two of grim effort. Romilar, like many other cough medicines, contains dextromethorphan hydrobromide, a chemical with hallucinogenic properties. Its recreational features are less well-known due to the quantities of sludge required for a threshold dose. In normal use, one or two teaspoons, it works well enough as a cough suppressant and mild sedative. By the pint, it becomes something else altogether, a slow-motion psychedelic carnival where movement and color melt into a soporific blur.

After a night of cherry-flavored delirium, I staggered to the induction center in time for the physical. However, I was in no shape for the Army, at least not that day, so they sent me home.

Three more weeks went by before I received another induction notice, but by that time, having fulfilled my duty to father and judge, I tore up the new draft card and took off. Maybe I was just a boy and the Army wanted to make a man out of me, but I decided that even if I never grew up, I would not meekly subject myself to fighting for an imperial cause. I had to draw a line somewhere.

8

The Frontier of Flesh & Stone

About halfway through high school, I figured out that my parents worried about me, concerned that I wasn't normal. They did accept a lot of my oddities: the constant reading, the writing, the fanzine publishing, the endless stream of letters and zines from all over the world, the radical politics, even my failures at bicycle riding and athletics in general. My father took me hunting and fishing for a while but stopped asking when I failed to show enthusiasm. I spent more time with my mother, playing cards, watching tv, and eating the endless parade of sugar-crammed treats she kept in stock. My faint interest in the standard manly things caused them to wonder if I was gay, a fear impossible to speak out loud.

I was bright; everyone said so, even though it was always mentioned as if to entail vague obligations. Getting good grades and pleasing my teachers went a long way to absolve my aberrations in the eyes of most adults. Still, throughout high school, there were no girlfriends. I got along with girls, talked with them, enjoyed their company, admired them. But I only had one date, and not until my senior year. By that time, I understood that I should be doing something pragmatic about the boy/girl thing, so I asked a classmate, a smart girl with intellectual ambitions and a disdain for popularity. We ended up in all the Honors classes together and due to alphabetical seating, I usually sat on her right and a little behind, a situation that allowed me to study her figure without being too obvious. We were friendly, so it made sense to ask her out: she was cute enough and, best of all, not one of the trendy kids, so she might be willing to be seen with someone like me. Even if she said no, I didn't imagine she would humiliate me by blabbing all over the school, or worse, do like a cheerleader did in junior high and smash a handful of popcorn into my face in front of a hundred kids.

She seemed pleased to accept the date, which immediately threw me off. Anticipating rejection, I wasn't prepared to move on to the next phase. All I knew about courting and intimate behavior had been learned from fiction. This included confusing material such as the swashbuckling conquests of Conan the Barbarian or the preposterous misogynies of *Stranger In A Strange Land*. I read Terry Southern's raunchy novel *Candy* and every now and then got a peek at *Playboy*. These kinds of things failed to give me any confidence of what I should do on a first date. My mother and I watched romantic Hollywood musicals together, which made her sing along and wriggle in her seat. However, since I could neither sing nor dance, I found nothing to emulate. No one took me aside and talked about sex, dating, courtship, or any of those things. My dad was too timid, and my mom certainly wasn't opening Pandora's Box. My geeky buddies didn't date much, either. And they didn't talk about it when they did, at least not to me. We didn't swap sexual lies and fantasies like a lot of other boys. Instead, we talked about music, books, board games, and how the hell we could get our hands on that LSD we kept hearing about. In short, I was ill prepared for romance.

The date was a sad affair. We went to a football game, a stupid idea, since neither one of us cared about football. When we took seats in the stands, I heard the other kids stifling snickers and making fun of us. Nothing too overt, all deniable, but unmistakable. We didn't acknowledge it, or each other, very much. Just sat in a kind of frightened paralysis until the game was over. I drove her back to her house, and didn't think about chatting in the car, a kiss, or a friendly touch. If we'd gone to a movie or out to dinner, we might have had fun, had a conversation, or even held hands. But I felt like a failure. I went home and assaulted my typewriter. Back in school, I had a hard time looking her in the eye. I decided to forget about dating.

When I dropped out of college and joined the brigades of hippies cluttering the streets, I wanted the drugs. The grandiosity of being in a counterculture added appeal, but for me, it was mostly about the drugs. According to the media, the culture was also loaded with sex. Everywhere you looked, women had stopped wearing bras, nudity was cool, and the love was free. That was the rumor, anyway. Outsiders assumed hippies had orgies all the time. It made for sensational press, but it wasn't like that. Some people were in relationships, some people played around, and some of us went without, like everywhere else.

Dedication to drugs nudged me into a mental monastery. I devoted myself to psychedelic ecstasy; physical love seemed unnecessary. Despite all the friendly women on the hippie scene, I was no better prepared to connect than I had been in high school. Less so, perhaps, because of the distractions that accompany constant drug use. Sex remained a theoretical construct.

Through no effort of my own, I met Gale on the streets of Seattle; she hung around with my friends clustered along the U District sidewalks, the hippie commons. I liked her looks and talked to her; no one else seemed particularly interested, though they tolerated her. I was pleased when she responded to my attention, and we spent a lot of time together. This went on for a few days, my first courtship, until we agreed to adjourn to the basement where I had a mattress. Our kissing and hugging and groping led to disrobing. She let me touch her wherever I wanted; the riches were intoxicating, and it was hard to know where to direct my attention. I knew that I was supposed to do something to her "down there;" that much I'd gleaned from my literary studies. Exposure to a lucid manual at some point would have helped me out, but my ignorance led to fumbling. She said nothing and waited passively for me to have my way with her. I would have been happy to oblige but I didn't know how. They say it's instinctual but I wonder. I tried for hours to unlock the secret of her pleasure without finding the key, an endeavor that led me from excitement to embarrassment and ended up in shame. She made a few half-hearted attempts to get me off but whatever spark had brought us to the basement had been snuffed. She was frustrated, and stated what she thought was proven fact: "You'll never be able to do it." I inhaled her prophecy as an oracle, an internal check on further experimentation. There wouldn't be much point, would there? I'd just been condemned to a life of celibacy.

Curiously, we didn't stop seeing each other, but continued to hang around the street, though without any effort toward sex. I supposed we liked each other, liked the talking, and maybe if there'd been some guidance, we could have learned to have a relationship. But there wasn't any; we were on our own. Soon, we drifted apart, reduced to a hello in passing. A year later I heard that Gale had died of a heroin overdose.

In the summer of 68, I went to New Mexico. Some Seattle friends were already there and when we rolled up after three days of driving, I stepped out of the car and staggered, light-headed. They lived in the town of Vallecitos at an elevation of 7500 ft. I'd never been that high; it was like someone sucked the air out of my lungs. We all gasped for a while and drank beer to quell the headaches. Then came the diarrhea. There was only one outhouse, and I didn't always make it in time. Too squeamish to wash my underwear, a job done by hand, I threw it away, accident after accident.

Our friends in New Mexico had recently been turned on to rock climbing, just like it was another drug. They insisted that we try it, right away. On day three they hauled us to a local cliff. A rush like no other, they said. We didn't have ropes, specialized shoes, or any sort of gear. It was one after another, scrambling up the vertical wall. "Grab that knob, there; stick your foot in the crack; don't look down; there's a ledge just above you; go for it!" No one fell, always a good thing. But they were right; the rush was intense. It was like giving the finger to death. I clenched every muscle in a mixture of fear and excitement, my bowels twisted into a constipated knot, and that ended the diarrhea.

Climbing was as intoxicating as any substance. We did it again, and again, and I caught the flame. Someone gave me a copy of Heinrich Harrer's *The White Spider*, an account of the 1938 first ascent of the Eiger north face. It was a bold climb, and Harrer, who was part of the team, milked the drama. He captured the daring in a harrowing narrative that soon became a beacon for dreamy, restless youth around the world. I read it, sweating over each page. It seemed as magical as any myth or fantasy quest—and it was real. I couldn't stop thinking about it, imagining my own mountain conquests.

By winter, I drifted back to Seattle, broke and homeless. I fed myself at a bohemian coffeehouse where I could purchase an overstuffed peanut butter and jelly sandwich for twenty-five cents, money I earned by begging on the street. The sandwich got me through, day-to-day, and when I discovered an old station wagon parked in the alley behind the coffeehouse, I recognized an opportunity. The back seat had been taken out and replaced with a mattress. I saw no current signs of occupation, so I moved in. I spent most of the winter there, warm enough in my Army surplus sleeping bag. During the day, I stood under awnings on the drizzly streets with the other denizens until I could swing an invitation to parties or bars where someone else would feed me and buy me drinks. It wasn't long until the dreams I had about climbing flickered in my thoughts like half-remembered films.

I improved my panhandling techniques, injecting humor into the patter, styling the performance to evoke a rascally but lovable tramp. Somehow this worked. In the evening I'd adjourn to a sleazy hippie bar where I spent the money tactically, first buying a pitcher of beer to share, then cruising the rest of the night on other people's pitchers. Alcohol was still the cheapest and easiest drug on the scene, and I relied on it more and more as a prescription for living. One night at the bar, after I'd been drinking several hours with friends, I was astonished to see Wendy walk in with two other women. The night we'd taken peyote together in New Mexico was a cherished memory, an image of what I'd decided was forever unattainable. She acted pleased to see me, squeezed in close, and commenced nuzzling in a way that left no doubt in my mind about her intentions. She was on her own now. I couldn't believe my luck. To celebrate I drank more beer, faster. Inevitably, I got absurdly drunk.

Wendy said she didn't like this bar; she usually avoided it. Understandable, it was filled with junkies and alcoholics. She was too glamorous for underworld pursuits; at least that was my fantasy about her. I'd also assumed that she was too glamorous for me, but her body told me something different. She suggested we go to a "nicer place," a trendy bar across town that I never visited because it was trendy. I ignored the cue, so she repeated it several times. Despite her touch and warm affection, I kept pouring down beers, lost in a fog of unreason. Finally, she and her friends got up to leave. She bent next to my ear and told me to come find her, which I thought was sweet.

I watched her leave, and the thought crossed my mind that I'd made a terrible mistake. No matter, I was drinking beer and by god, that's what I was going to do. The neon and noise of the bar erased regret. When the open-eyed swirlies hit, I had to bolt. I staggered into the alley and unloaded my guts. Under the night drizzle, I retched and retched, prone on the asphalt. I couldn't get up so I lay there, stunned, with the taste of vomit in my mouth. A junkie I knew came slinking down the alley, no doubt on the way to retrieve the heroin he'd hidden before entering the bar. I was in the way, so he stepped over me, pausing in sympathy, "Oh man, bummer, can't find your stash…?" I moaned in response, but he wasn't really interested in my plight; he had his own.

I never saw Wendy again, which was just as well. If I had, I would have burned to the ground in shame.

After that, things went further downhill. Alcohol is a cruel master and I surrendered completely. Dark pains that I'd never named emerged from cracks in my mind and crawled over me like maggots on a corpse. What had started in multi-colored psychedelic splendor had squandered its hues for a washed-out charcoal gray. If there was a bottom yet to reach, it would be hard, terminally hard. I thought that's what I wanted, or maybe just to flirt with it and it'd turn out all right in the end. I had no fucking clue.

Here and there, it had occurred to me that maybe I wanted to do something in life besides annihilate myself. Even the occasional thought kept the question alive. Unfortunately, I lacked the volition to improve my lot and existed day to day. In a moment of lucidity, I bummed enough change to buy food, a surplus rucksack, and a raincoat, and I headed to the mountains, the North Cascades. It was simple enough, just hitchhike out of Seattle and get off at a trailhead in the forest, then start walking. The trails always led uphill. At timberline, I'd leave the marked paths and wander across the ridges and meadows of the high country, a place where you could get some perspective. It gave me peace, and enough vantage to catch glimpses of myself. I decided that at the age of 19 there might be a few benefits left to gain from living; it was naïve, downright premature, to give up already.

After several more high-country rambles, off-trail and always alone, I decided to go back to New Mexico. By this time, our friends had moved away from Vallecitos to the larger village of El Rito, at 6800 ft. still rarefied, but on the margin between the mountains and the high desert. They'd rented an enormous adobe house with a wraparound porch and a grove of peach trees. Tubbs showed me to a room with an extra mattress where I could sleep. The room was spacious and featured a long, wide table covered with climbing equipment: carabiners, pitons, hammers, slings, ropes, rock shoes, and a small stack of mountain magazines. The carabiners and pitons were laid in rows of like after like, or in the case of the pitons, in gradations of size. Everything was placed with the obsessive precision of a fetish. We stood around the table and talked climbing while Tubbs, Drone, and White showed off the objects with pride. It seemed excessive, but I couldn't resist picking up the carabiners and clicking the gates open and shut, open and shut.

I felt honored to bed down in the space of the sacred gear. Before sleep, I lit a kerosene lamp and read the magazines. That's where I learned about Yosemite. *The White Spider* celebrated an alpine ethos, the world of mountain ice and remote peaks thousands of miles and an ocean away, unattainable for unemployed drug bums in America. But Yosemite was something different. It was a mecca of pure rock, right in California, and you could climb year-round. A tempting notion, but it was the photographs that blew my mind. Huge granite cliffs towered into blue skies in formations that seemed to be archetypes of the divine, more perfect than Greek temples. As I read and stared at the images, the idea burned a hole in me: I had to go there. I had to.

When we weren't babbling obsessively about climbing, we were trying to cope with life in the desert. The venomous ecosystem kept us alert to hazards. In Vallecitos, the black widow spiders not only lurked in the corners but in the shady areas of our minds. After moving to El Rito, Tubbs implemented a management scheme. He captured the spiders and kept them in mason jars on top of the bookshelf. For amusement, he'd introduce a new spider to the jar of a veteran and watch them fight to the death. The victors received prizes of dead flies. I told him he was fucking nuts. He laughed but pointed out that every spider in a jar was one less spider roaming the house.

A persistent stream of visitors appeared at the El Rito house, a mixture of Seattle friends and New Mexico locals. They all wanted to party. Lots of weed and booze, and whatever they brought with them. It wasn't what you'd call a stable household. One drunken evening somebody chucked an empty bottle across the living room. It crashed into the jars full of Tubbs' spiders, resulting in broken glass and scrambling arachnids. Tubbs happened to be standing nearby and rushed over to pound his fists on the shelf. He pounded like a wild man, screaming while he went at it. I turned off the music and Tubbs held up his fists. Blood streamed down his arms, and I could see fragments of crushed spider parts and glass shards. "No way did I want those fuckers running loose in the house; those were the champions, the baddest of the bad!" His wisdom was irrefutable. Somebody gave him a beer and I turned the music back on.

Toward the end of summer, three women arrived from Seattle. One of them knew somebody, I don't remember who. Single women were a precious commodity in our mostly male environment; three at once was a windfall. A quick shuffle decided the attachments for two of them, but not the third. No one wanted her; she was plump and plain. Her name was Nausicaa, she said. I'm embarrassed to admit that I didn't recognize the source of this unusual name, but it escaped me. It made me think of "nausea." But that had nothing to do with it, except in my sour imagination. Whether by her parents, or self-selected, her namesake was a princess, the one praised by Homer, who told the story of how royal Nausicaa found Odysseus washed up on the beach after another one of his shipwrecks. You can read about it in Book Six of *The Odyssey*. According to the bard, she is a lovely, eligible young woman, graceful in manner, endearing herself to the reader as well as Odysseus.

The Seattle Nausicaa read the room, picked me out and homed in like a pigeon ready to roost. She followed me around, trying to converse and make friends. Since no one wanted her, I couldn't encourage her overtures and kept trying to slip away. But Nausicaa was at least as determined as her namesake. Unannounced, she eased into my bed early in the night. I was surprised but offered no resistance. Her touch felt good, and she knew what to do. It didn't matter that I was inexperienced; she directed our encounter with authority. We coupled easily and all the anxieties of my unfulfilled desires washed away in the baptism. She snuggled by my side, and I wondered why I had scorned this woman. Was I that shallow? Apparently, since I didn't get past the wondering and dropped into a deep, satisfied sleep, snoring like a freight train.

Nausicaa and her friends left the next day, leaving me with the one lesson. For a long time, I didn't appreciate how lucky I had been to meet someone so patient and gentle.

A few weeks later, I hitched to Yosemite for the fall season. Although it cooled off at night, the October days were warm and sunny, ideal for climbing in "the Valley," as everyone called it. I went straight to Camp 4, the climber's camp, a tent-only area, which resembled a festival of bohemian nomads. Clusters of tents occupied each camp site like ad hoc family groups. I didn't know anyone, but I walked around and was soon invited to join a site. If you had a rope lashed to your pack, people recognized you as another seeker who had made the pilgrimage. You were respected for that alone. The Valley did feel like a sacred place. Everywhere you looked, you saw majesty. Idyllic meadows outlined by giant oak and pine trees flanked the course of the Merced River, providing superb nooks for picnics and naps. Each side of the flat-bottomed valley was bounded by vertical granite walls of staggering size. The rock itself was hard and clean, colored in mineralized pastels, tapestries of lithic art. Awestruck, I could tell other climbers by the way they walked around, necks craning, heads tilted back, staring up at the ultimate rock-climbing paradise. Just to be there inspired worship.

It was mostly men in Camp 4, young men. A few women climbed and a few girlfriends stayed in the camp. But they were a minority. As a result, the camp could have been an outdoor locker room for monks. Climbers smoked dope and drank, played chess, laughed and dallied if they had the chance, but everyone was a fanatic in their devotion to climbing. You had to be. Pull-up bars and slack lines were lashed between trees and working out was a part of the routine. Despite being surrounded by relaxing wild beauty, the denizens were hyper-focused. This was the place. The best climbers in the world came here to test themselves. Bragging rights were a drug. There was room for the average or beginning climber, too, on the walls and in the fraternity, but you couldn't go a day without seeing or hearing about somebody doing something that had never been done before. This was the Big Time.

My shelter was an orange plastic tube tent that cost ten bucks and wasn't worth a penny more. I pitched it between two pine trees and sat down at the picnic table with my new companions. We passed a joint and got acquainted. I could see these guys liked to get high, but not stupid; the goals were athletic and required a healthy body. It didn't take long for me to realize the shortcomings of shoveling drugs into my body for the previous two years. I needed to get in shape. My camp mates tipped me off that I could get food for free in the park employees' cafeteria. Just walk in, buy a coffee, sit down, and when the employees were done with their meal, slide over and grab their plates. The employees didn't care; the meals were included in their contract, and to them, the food was so awful nobody could eat a whole plate of it. Hungry climbers were less discriminating. The employees found it amusing and once they knew you by sight, would even secure extra portions.

I went on some easy climbs with a couple of the guys I met in camp. I'd learned rope and protection techniques in New

Mexico, and we'd practiced on the cliffs there, but Yosemite climbers were on the cutting edge of technique and there was a lot to learn. It was a perfect place to study. Every day was sunny, temperatures ran in the sixties and low seventies, and the landscape of the Valley made me feel like I had stepped through a portal into a dream.

After a month of Camp 4, I was in the best physical shape of my life. All the exercise and clean air wrung the crap out of my system. When my friend White showed up from New Mexico, I felt ready to push some limits. His name was Mike White, but everyone called him either "mikewhite" like it was one word, or just plain "White." Even though he'd done more than his share of heroin and self-abuse, he was a natural athlete and he loved to climb. I figured we could get ambitious.

We had dreams, but I knew we weren't ready for a big wall. Those were the multi-day Grade VI routes that grabbed the headlines, like the ones on the formidable cliff known as El Capitan. That was unthinkable. But stoked on my own passion, I convinced him we could do the Grade III Direct Route on Washington Column. The climb was rated 5.7, which meant that there were no moves on the route harder than stuff we'd already done. It would be technical, but not difficult. What I ignored in my eagerness was the Grade III label. It would be a long climb, twelve pitches or so, well over a thousand feet, which might take a whole day or close to it. I hadn't climbed anything longer than three pitches and White had never done more than one. It still seemed like something we could do. None of our friends had done a climb on that scale, so, at least within our circle, there would be bragging rights.

It looked steep from the base. The whole formation resembled a prow of rock jutting into the valley. Our route ascended the round side of the prow, where it intersected the long wall of slab cliffs known as Royal Arches. From this angle, it really did look like a column, one suitable for a temple of the gods. It seemed huge, like everything in the Valley, and we couldn't wait to start. We figured we'd make it to the top in plenty of time to find the trail back down on the other side of the prow. We only brought the bare necessities: one rope, pitons, hammer, a few slings and carabiners. I wore a light sweater due to the cool morning. White, a tough guy, had his tee shirt and said he was fine. I led the first pitch, easy scrambling up cracks and slabs that gradually steepened. I stopped at a narrow ledge and studied the next section, the crux, where the hardest climbing would be found. The sunlight reflected off the crystals in the granite, illuminating the wall above me, highlighting its clean cracks and knobby surfaces. It beckoned with a promise of beautiful climbing, the kind that lured people to Yosemite. I wanted to lead it, but I wanted my friend to understand that everything he'd heard about the Valley was true.

I belayed White as he climbed to my stance. He removed the pitons as he followed the rope, and when he joined me, I encouraged him to lead the next one. This was common practice, to swing leads up a route. It's more efficient and saves the time of swapping the belay. He nodded and started up the face. Less than twenty feet above me, he paused, then started a sequence of moves to where he could place the next piton for protection, got partway there, then reversed back to his stance. He tried again. And again. Up, up, then back down. I didn't see what his problem was but started yelling advice anyway. He looked down at me and said okay. Not the next try, but the one after, he made it, hammered in a piton, and stopped to catch his breath. He pushed on, jamming his rock shoes and one hand into the crack while the other hand grabbed knobs on the face, using his already shaking muscles to extend his body upward. One foot slipped out of the crack, he swore and climbed down to the rest point below the piton.

The sun was warm on the face, but it wasn't hot. Perfect, really. I continued to yell encouragement and advice, urging him on. It was inconceivable to me that he couldn't do it. Yet every inch was a struggle for him. He kept going up one or two moves, then back down to the last secure foothold. He started to thrash instead of climb, trying to will himself up the rock. Despite the evidence of my eyes, I refused to believe that he wasn't going to be able to lead the pitch. In New Mexico, he'd been a better climber than me; he was always the biggest and strongest of us all.

Finally, he asked me to hold him on a tight rope and he climbed back down to the belay stance. "I can't do it," he said. That's not an easy thing to admit, and I wasn't sure I really agreed with him. But something had to change. I shrugged and took over the lead. The pitch went smoothly enough; the climbing didn't seem that hard. Sure, it was a puzzle, figuring out the correct sequence of moves, but not tricky. I set up a belay and yelled for White to follow. We'd used up a lot of time on that pitch. Too much time. Hours, apparently. Other difficulties lay ahead of us, according to the route guide, maybe not as hard as the crux, but probably too hard for White. I'd have to lead all the way, or we'd never get up.

He agreed to this plan; I thought he'd be insulted, but he looked relieved. He didn't seem to have trouble following the pitches, but it's true, leading is different. In following, the rope is above you and if you fall, you're not going very far, maybe just an inch or two; it's a secure feeling. Leading, though, the rope is below you, pulled up through carabiners attached to pitons hammered in the cracks. You're always climbing above your last point of protection and if you fall, you're falling twice that far. There's a motto in the climbing world: the leader doesn't fall. With good reason, leader falls can be spectacular, and not in a good way. That's why they call it the sharp end of the rope.

The route was named direct for a reason; it headed nearly straight up the cliff, connecting vertical cracks with small traverses. It wasn't hard climbing by Valley standards, but it was vertical and not exactly easy, either. Belays had to be fixed on ledges barely big enough for standing, let alone sitting, and as we ascended, the valley floor receded below us until the tops of the giant conifers resembled the shrubbery in a model train set.

I pushed the pace as best I could, but after ten pitches, we ran out of time. The sun gave up on the day and dropped below the horizon and we were still a couple of pitches from the top. I'd just arrived at a ledge about the size of a small bench. With care, the two of us could sit side by side. It seemed prudent to stop rather than try to finish the climb in the dark. Without flashlights or headlamps, it'd be easy to make a serious mistake. All we had to do was get through the night on the ledge and finish up in the morning; simple enough. We hammered a couple of pitons into a crack in the wall and lashed ourselves to them. The air temperature cooled rapidly. White only had the tee shirt on top, but for some reason I didn't understand, he had long johns under his pants. He removed the long johns and pulled them on over his head, forcing his skull through the crotch. He invited me to jeer at him, but I didn't have the heart. Sometimes you do what you have to do. I wrapped loops of rope around my legs, hoping that would hold in a little heat.

With our backs pressed flat against the wall, if we straightened our legs, everything below the knee dangled over the edge, a thousand feet to the bottom. We watched lights go on in the Valley as the various lodges offered evening dining and activities for the tourists. There was no moon, and when the sky faded into blackness, the stars revealed themselves, first by the hundreds, then thousands, then, I was sure, by the millions. It was a brilliant spectacle; one that I'd have all night to contemplate. I pulled my knees to my chest and rewrapped the rope. Neither of us had a watch; we measured the night by the turning of the heavens and the falling temperature. It got very cold. We huddled shoulder-to-shoulder and shivered. There wasn't much to say to each other. We had no food or water, not even a joint to smoke. We sat on the wall and stared into space, helpless to prevent our vitality from being sucked into the void.

Impossible to sleep, of course, or even doze off. Shudders rippled through us as we fought hypothermia. I watched the eastern horizon, repeatedly thinking I saw the gray of pre-dawn, and if I didn't see it, then I tried to conjure it into existence. But the world didn't respond. We were two impetuous fools sitting on the throne of consequences.

When dawn came, I'd burned through all the remnants of magical thinking. As the sunlight filled the sky, it was time to get off the wall. During the night of rumination, I'd convinced myself that we'd gone off-route. That was why we didn't get to the top; instead of cruising up the moderate pitches at the end, we'd been climbing some harder variant. I couldn't see it any other way. The crack system continued up from the ledge, though, and would probably take us to the top if we could follow it for another two hundred feet. White and I looked at each other through the eyes of exhaustion. The night had taken more out of us than the day of climbing, and the combination left us weak and vanquished. I studied the crack above. Whatever mojo I had the day before was gone; this just looked hard and dangerous. "I can't do it," I said, joining the club of defeat.

"Shit," said White.

"Let's try a traverse around to the gully, maybe there's an easier way up."

He wasn't going to argue; at this point, it was my show, whatever was left of it. While White belayed, I climbed horizontally to the left, using holds and cracks wherever I could find them. Anxiously, I surveyed the wall above me, looking for an easy crack or some kind of weakness in the façade. I found nothing like that. In the gully, the angle was lower, until it ended below a huge overhang. Trees grew above the lip of the overhang; that would be the end of the climb. But the overhang looked insurmountable, not something I'd take on, ever. Below me, the gully was filled with sand and gravel from crumbled rock. Ball bearings, the perfect accelerant to a plunge.

I belayed White over to my stance. "I guess we need to rappel," I said. He was game; it meant no more upward exertion. Sliding down the rope seemed like something we could manage.

We wouldn't be able to claim credit for the climb, but I didn't see any scenario where we made the summit, not after that night. Rappelling all the way down the face gave me pause, though. Only two weeks before, I'd been strolling around the smaller cliffs along the Valley floor, chatting with a new friend, when we heard a sickening crunch behind us. We hurried back to find a young man crumpled at the base of a cliff, tangled in ropes. He groaned faintly and died. His partner came running down the backside of the cliff, but it was too late for anyone to do anything. They'd been practicing rappels and had tied into an old anchor, a weathered sling. When it broke, the guy fell a hundred feet. Most climbing accidents happen on descents and rappelling is probably the single most dangerous maneuver. Everything depends on your gear and your set-up. If anything fails, hanging from the rope becomes a plummet to the bottom.

White and I faced a thousand feet of rappels. We'd have to fix an anchor with a sling, thread the rope through the sling to the halfway point, throw the length down the cliff and slide down the doubled rope, retrieving it by pulling on a free end. Then we'd set the next anchor, and so forth, down the wall. Most climbers take two ropes, one to climb on, the other as a backup and utility line. Because we couldn't afford two, we only had one length of 120 feet. That meant the longest rappel we could manage would be 60 feet. We were looking at a lot of rappels.

We had a minimal number of pitons and slings. Each rappel anchor, if it was going to be solid enough to take our weight, one after the other, would cost at least one piece of gear. There would be no retrieving these anchors once we were at the other end of the rope. No question about it, going down was going to cost us everything we had. But the anchors had to be solid; no way I wanted to hear that crunch again. Let alone feel it.

We rapped straight down the side of the column. At each new set, we scanned the wall below, anxious to ensure that the rappel would arrive at a ledge and not in space. We tied a knot at the end of the rope, just in case, because we'd heard the stories about people sliding off the ends. Like a lot of mistakes in climbing, you don't get a second chance. We were exhausted, but it was no time to get sloppy. One rappel led to another, and we slowly descended the face. Each anchor cost a piton and a sling. Sometimes we landed at a ledge big enough to harbor a small tree, and we used that instead. We fretted about it and tried to be conservative, but that didn't stop us from running out of gear. Two-thirds of the way down, we ended at a ledge and had nothing left. There was a conifer, a seedling really, that had forged a toehold for itself in a crack. It curved upward and we could loop the rope around it, no slings needed. We both tested it, dismayed by its springiness, by its flimsy, foolish attempt to find a perch in vertical granite. It was only slightly thicker than my thumb. It seemed absolute madness to use it. But there was nothing else. I fixed the rappel and put my weight on it, watching it flex under the burden. Down I went, clenched in fear. I got to another ledge and unclipped from the rope. White slid down and we pulled the rope after him, looking at each other the way people do when they know they're cheating death and understanding that, at some point, there would be no more cheating.

Lower on the wall, there were ledges with shrubs and fledgling trees more than adequate for anchors. Fourteen rappels later, we came to low-angle slabs easy enough for scrambling without a rope. By mid-afternoon we stood on the pine-needle carpet of the Valley floor.

"We can't tell anyone about this, ever," White said. He was embarrassed. I understood that; there was nothing to brag about. He'd been unable to lead a single pitch and had to follow along like a duffer. Not only that, but we'd ended up bivouacking on a day climb. And if that wasn't enough, we hadn't even made it to the top. From his perspective, the whole thing was a failure.

I took that away as well. While we struggled with a beginner's route, other climbers in the Valley were putting up the hardest and most challenging rock climbs in the world, the stuff filling the pages of climbing journals. The exploits were daring. Technical rock mastery had been pushed to a new rating level, 5.11, and the understanding of what could be done had changed. Meanwhile, we couldn't even finish a 5.7. It was humiliating. But for me, there was something else. Number one, we'd survived. Secondly, I'd shown some toughness. Hardly hero material, but I surprised myself with how I handled the situation. For perhaps the first time in my life, I had been a leader, a guide. What was that about?

9

Friction

Compatible rock-climbing partners are not easy to find. Basically, you want somebody with equivalent skill who understands the importance of holding your rope and taking turns. Friendship doesn't always translate to the vertical world. It's not like you're spending the afternoon on the porch over tea; the main conversation you'll have during the climb involves shouted directions about rope management and brief encouragement when switching belays. Mistakes can only be forgiven if you survive. What this boils down to is that you don't even have to like the guy at the other end of the rope, not as long as he takes care of his half of the bargain. I didn't appreciate this nuance of climbing relations until I met Damon at Indian Rock in Berkeley. I bouldered on the outcrops almost every day, we watched each other climb, and eventually, we started talking. Let's do some real walls, he proposed. I agreed. But not Yosemite. It's winter—too cold. I've got a car, he said, let's go to Tahquitz Rock. In the mountains east of LA, four hundred warmer miles south, it was a long way, but he had a car, so why not? We agreed to go, one of these days, and reminded each other every time we crossed paths.

I'd been hanging around Berkeley for a few months during the fall of 70. Aside from the daily sojourn to Indian Rock, I walked the streets and wondered how much longer I could live without a reliable income. I crashed with my high school friend Alan in his apartment. After the first few days, his girlfriend pretended I didn't exist. I slept on a cot in the entrance hall and wasn't allowed past the kitchen. Alan worked at the Berkeley Barb, an underground newspaper that erupted into fame in the mid-60s before spinning out of control like every other underground journal. He did layouts and typesetting, a regular job. Since I claimed to be a writer, he got me a freelance gig. I could sit in the news office and use a typewriter to hammer out stories that pretended to be journalism but were just opinions and anecdotes. The staff never edited or questioned my articles; they just printed them. At one time the paper had national influence, but in the realm of media, influence and quality don't always exist on the same page. A solid third of the Barb consisted of explicit ads for escort services, sex shops, sex books, and everything else related to sex that could be bought and sold. My articles inevitably showed up framed in bare bottoms and pendulous breasts, all arranged by Alan, proud to highlight his friend's prose in lurid counterpoint.

One day, I was sitting at a typewriter working on a possible masterpiece about the Alianza movement in New Mexico when the editor-in-chief marched into the newsroom and announced, "Ok, let's go, we're shutting down. Leave whatever you're doing, grab your belongings and get out. I'm locking up in five minutes." And that was the end of the Berkeley Barb, at least until somebody else bought it and tried again to make it work. You could hardly call it a job, but now that it was over, it seemed like time to take Damon up on his offer of Tahquitz Rock. When I packed my belongings, Alan's girlfriend broke her silence to offer a hopeful goodbye.

I didn't actually like Damon. He talked too much, argued about everything, proclaimed wild opinions, and seemed to have misplaced his moral compass—all the makings of a shifty character. He had long, unwashed hair, a scruffy beard, and looked like a guy who'd been living under an overpass, feral and unpredictable. Not that I appeared different. If you were playing the part of a dirtbag climbing bum, it was important to look like one. But that didn't curtail my scorn. Damon didn't like me either, at least that's what I derived from his sarcasm and glaring, needlepoint eyes. Despite these antipathies, we climbed together in harmony. When we tied to the rope and alternated leads, finding our way up a rock face, we belayed each other faithfully, ascending in a state of grace, like dancers flying through music. As soon as we got off the rock, then the bickering started again. It was a partnership of split personalities.

Luckily, Damon had a bag of weed, which helped us chill out during the trip south. While he drove, I made peanut butter sandwiches from the provisions I'd bought with my last check as a journalist. Excited for the adventure, we abandoned the usual abrasive dialogue and just smoked joints and ate sandwiches.

Tahquitz Rock soared above the town of Idylwild, a mountain suburb common to Southern California. Big city money, mostly. We drove through town late in the afternoon, awed by the surrounding rock walls, wondering where and how to find our niche in this granite paradise. We needed free lodging. Motels or campground fees, parking fees, anything like that was out of the question. A place to pitch a tent would suffice. Damon and I had the same background; we were used to the rules of camping in the National Forests of the Pacific Northwest, which meant that there weren't any rules, and if there were, they weren't enforced. The land belonged to the nation; it was there for you and me, just like the man said. We ignored the prolific signs around Idylwild about don't do this or don't do that and drove out of town, turned up a gravel road, and crossed the boundary into the San Jacinto Wilderness Area. Federal land, we were home free.

Damon parked on the shoulder, well off the road. About half a mile away towered the monolithic pyramid of Tahquitz. We threw tents, sleeping bags, and the food we had into our packs and hiked up through the pines. We walked until we found an open area in the forest with level ground to pitch our tents. From there it was an easy hike across the slope to the cliffs, a reasonable approach.

The next morning, we got on the rock early. We climbed granite so perfect it seemed like a dream. Cracks were clean and solid, and the rugged surface of the rock provided a friction of adherence that worked like magic. Our partnership of rope unspooled with telepathic ease. We even smiled at each other once or twice. By afternoon we were tired and hungry, so we hiked back to our camp to cook a pot of brown rice. We'd brought a five-pound bag and dried soup mixes to throw in for flavor. Spartan, perhaps, but if you smoked some weed, it was good enough.

We gathered downed branches from among the pines, laid out rocks in a ring, and argued about the best way to start a fire. Since Damon had the matches, he won. After he wasted a couple trying to strike them on the worn-out box, I impressed him with my one-handed technique of lighting a wooden match on my thumbnail. He hung an aluminum pot from a propped stick, and we kicked back to wait for the rice to boil. Afternoon shadows grew long by the time we finished our meal and sat around the fire, feeding it extra sticks, and watching the flames. The glow from our day of climbing filled us with good cheer and we failed to find anything more to argue about. Instead, we sat in contented silence.

When the hackles on my neck told me something wasn't right, I looked up to see half a dozen men closing in from three directions. They all clutched shovels like weapons. Alarmed, I jumped up to face their advance. They fixed us with angry glares and ran to the fire, scooping dirt on the flames and kicking the stones away. One of them had a water pack and sprayed the coals as if determined to eradicate from the earth every vestige of combustion.

"Is this your fire?" A guy in olive brown khakis and a dark brown windbreaker stood in front of us. He wore a baseball cap with an official patch, a ranger insignia; I was too freaked out to read it. He wasn't remotely friendly. I admitted that it was our fire.

"You're under arrest," he said.

"What?" I wasn't sure I heard him correctly.

For Damon, however, someone flicked a switch. "Fascist motherfuckers!" He shouted it three times, casting a spell. The guy looked at Damon like he was a squashable bug.

"What's the charge?" I needed clarification.

"No campfires allowed, period. Our lookout spotted the smoke," he motioned to one of the men burying the smoldering remnants of our crime. "What are you two, anyway: hobos? Never mind, save it for the judge. Maybe he cares. Let's go."

He let us pack up our gear, then they marched us down to the road and we locked our stuff in Damon's trunk. They never saw the weed, a good thing; it would have spiked our threat level.

The ranger's truck looked like a cop vehicle, with a caged back seat. That was my introduction to a different type of forest ranger, not the friendly, helpful guidebook ranger, but the backwoods enforcer, the guy who makes sure miscreants toe the line and if they don't, he busts them without remorse. As I soon learned, few crimes in Southern California were as heinous as starting a fire. Coming from the Pacific Northwest, where the woods were wet and you had to summon Prometheus himself to get a fire going, I had no inkling of the devastating history of fires in this area. You didn't start a fire anywhere in this region, not if you wanted to avoid being lynched by property owners. In fact, as he claimed, the ranger had probably done us a favor with the arrest.

Within an hour we were installed in Riverside County Jail. It was Friday evening, so we'd have to spend the weekend until we could see the judge on Monday. Meanwhile, we were marched into a common holding cell. They called it a cell, but it was more like barracks, a large cage containing about fifty bunkbeds lined up in rows with narrow aisles. Damon took a low bunk, and I climbed above him. Except for us, every inmate was Latino. I'd lived a few months in New Mexico, so I wasn't overwhelmed by the racial disparity. Regardless, I tried to stay quiet and offend no one. My goal was to lay on the bunk and speak only if necessary. Pulling that off required that I pretend Damon wasn't below me, muttering, cursing, and raging against the fascist pig motherfucking state.

As the evening went on, every bunk in the cell filled up. Even that didn't stop the forces of law and order. They kept bringing them in, at first letting them drag a mattress to sleep in the aisles, or when those were full, to let them hunch on the floor with their backs against the bars. Hard to imagine what was going on in the city to merit all these incarcerations. Maybe Damon was right about the fascist state, especially if you were the wrong color.

I guess most of us were in for similar things: petty crimes, the kinds of things that happen in the off-hours, accompanied by revelry, where human beings rub against each other, sparks fly, and violence or vandalism degrades the social order. I'd be surprised if anyone else was in there for a campfire, though.

Jail time is often portrayed in films as treacherous or uncomfortably relational, an interruption from life where you pump iron and get victimized. It can be like that. Mostly, though, it's boring. There is literally nothing to do but wait for the next meal. If you have cigarettes, you're golden. These days you can't smoke in prison, but in 1970 you were expected to. I never smoked tobacco until I went to jail. I saw the value of it right away and gladly accepted when the guy on the bunk across the aisle gave me one. Maybe it was a reward for keeping quiet, unlike Damon and several other loudmouths. Nobody likes a troublemaker, least of all in jail where you can't get away from them. I stayed on my bunk and looked at the ceiling.

On Monday morning, they took us to court. We sat together at the defendant's table and the judge asked me how I pled. I saw no reason to pretend that we weren't caught red-handed burning sticks in the woods. "Guilty," I said.

When the judge asked Damon the same question, he leaped up and raved like a lunatic. More crap about fascists, how everybody in the court room was a fascist, how the state had gone too far, how his rights were being trampled, and a bunch of other stuff, all containing references to "fucking fascists." He used big gestures and a loud voice. I cringed and tried to sink into my chair, thinking they would drag him out of there, or maybe both of us for good measure. The judge pounded his gavel and asked Damon again how he pled. He pointed out that if he opted for trial and couldn't make bail, then he'd return to Riverside Jail in the meantime. That shut Damon up. "Guilty," he said, snarling.

We received fifty-dollar fines. Since we'd been incarcerated over the weekend, the state called it square. We were free to go.

Hitching back to Idyllwild to get the car, Damon kept up a constant diatribe. I fumed but kept silent. I was sick of his bullshit. Still, by the time we got to the car, he'd calmed down and the memories of our excellent climbing partnership took over. We drove away from Idyllwild and along dirt roads deep into the wilderness, ending up high on top of a ridge. We camped there and ate peanut butter sandwiches, no fires. Each day, we'd throw our sleeping bags in the trunk and drive down to climb on the cliffs of Tahquitz Rock.

It was glorious, beautiful climbing. The freedom contrasted nicely with the days in jail. During the evening, we'd sit around and make preposterous plans for alpine adventures all over the world. But the truth was, when Damon dropped me off in Berkeley, I never wanted to see the motherfucker again.

10

Unsuitable

By 1971 I'd cut back on my consumption of psychedelics. Now and then, I'd indulge when the circumstances were right. If someone offered a vintage tab manufactured by this or that underground cult chemist, sure. Saying no would be like declining a wafer blessed by the pope. But I didn't hunger for it. I'd followed the road of the psychonaut, but after passing through the visions, I ended up staring at an empty horizon. Malaise filled my heart, yet I couldn't name it or interpret why it was there. Climbing had given me a focus, just not much in the way of understanding. True, I'd learned a few things in the mountains. The realities of rock and ice and the hard matter of the physical world took me outside of myself, an antidote to psychedelic introspection.

Still, the underlying problems were the same: I didn't know who I was, who I wanted to be, or who I could be. Even if someone knew the answers to those questions, I didn't know how to ask them. Instead, doubts coursed through me in a loud stream, drowning everything else.

With no other ideas, I went to the mountains. I wasn't a very good climber, that had become obvious, even though I wished otherwise. I'd always wanted to be the best at something, but it wasn't going to be that. I settled for the rewards of the landscape itself: the precipitous, jagged peaks, the frozen tongues of ice, the sensual alpine meadows with their heather and whistling marmots, the sensation of being in the air, above the world.

That summer, as the snowpack melted, I took a week long solo scramble along the alpine ridges surrounding Mt. Shuksan in the North Cascades. I had a rucksack, a tarp, a sleeping bag, and a cheap down jacket. For food I ate nuts, raisins, goat cheese, and dense rye bread, nothing cooked. Water was gathered from rills and tarns. The idea was to go light with minimal gear and bivouac wherever I ended up at the end of the day. I followed my eyes, wandering over outcrops and through meadows, a flaneur of the heights. When I got to a place that felt right, a welcoming place such as a sweet, grassy ledge on the edge of a cliff, I'd make a nest and watch the light diminish into the west. I didn't have a method, not consciously, but now I understand; I emptied my mind and let it refill with the elements of a perfect world. My goals for eating psychedelic drugs had been similar, but the chemical visions and sensations, in the end, were only manifestations of my interior; they added little to the quest for meaning.

At the time, my narratives were flimsy and I followed unconscious impulses, searching for something I couldn't articulate. I only understood that in the mountains, alone, I felt moments of integration. If I belonged nowhere else, I felt at home with the wind-scoured architecture of the alpine world.

The view from on high provided a moment of clarity, but that environment wasn't a place to settle down and dwell. To live there, you needed fur and a burrow. My limit was a week or two at most, then it was back to the lowlands. About three days into my Shuksan sojourn, the inevitable storm advanced out of the west like an aerial tidal wave. I hiked down before it swamped the ridges with snow and rain. Lacking any other pertinent destination, I hitchhiked across the state to my parents' house. I hadn't seen them in a while, and I knew they would feed me and let me sleep in my old bed. They worried about me, especially my mother, and not without justification. She'd be glad to see me and wouldn't press too hard on the obvious concern about what I was doing with my life. No, we'd focus on neutral stuff. My dad might take me rock hunting in the desert and my mother would enjoy having an ally to watch tv. Going home was like taking a break from trying to be an adult. After a while, I'd get restless, but it was okay for a spell.

As soon as I got home, my mom told me about the wiretap. After the fiasco in Louisiana, they had learned the details of my failure to be inducted into the Army. My fugitive method didn't please them, but they agreed with the object: to stay out of Vietnam. The carnage and confusion of that war occupied the national discourse. It seemed senseless to many who served in WWII, where the enemy was global and the threats were undeniable. It took a lot of rhetoric to argue for the intervention in SE Asia. And it was difficult for Americans to accept that despite the sacrifices, we were not winning. Kids were dying and parents didn't understand why. My mother, who never slept well, said that one night she watched someone climb the telephone pole behind the house. The next day and from then on, every time she picked up the phone, unusual clicks could be heard, as if activating another line. She was pretty sure it had to do with me, and she didn't like it one bit. Even my cautious father agreed. They were outraged at being the subjects of surveillance.

It had been almost four years since I received my first draft notice. I'd been running ever since, except for the time they caught up with me, and then, as soon as I could, I ran again. It wasn't just that I didn't want to get killed in combat, I was dead set against the whole military program. Even though I'd grown up on a diet of blood-thirsty heroic fantasies and Icelandic sagas, I couldn't imagine doing such things myself. I was meek, willing to turn my cheeks like a good pacifist. My secret hero was the Vietnamese monk who sat on a public square in lotus pose, drenched in gasoline, and lit himself on fire. He didn't flinch as the flames wreathed his body and consumed his life. Forget Achilles, Conan, and Egil Skallagrimsson, the monk had tapped into a power beyond common understanding. I wasn't that brave, but I could be stubborn. No matter what, I wasn't going to war.

If I wanted to stay ahead of the FBI, I knew I had to be careful. Risky behaviors had led to my first arrest by the feds. After that, I tried to keep a lower profile. I knew there was another federal warrant because I'd received the mail dutifully forwarded by my parents to a general delivery address. I never stayed in one place for more than a month or two. There was a risk in going to see my folks; I knew that. Still, I didn't know what else to do. I felt like a failure at life, lacking direction and means. A week or two at home would give me the energy to try again. Or so I hoped.

My mother stuffed me with food three times a day and urged snacks on me at points between. In the evening, I'd play cribbage with my father while we sipped on his homemade raspberry wine. They loved me, a fact I could hardly understand. All their endeavors at parenting must have seemed futile, yet there I was, still their son, still belonging. I tried to soak it up because I knew it couldn't last. We could pretend, but I wasn't really their little boy anymore.

I'd been there for a week, eating, sleeping, and taking long showers, when one day I heard a knock at the door. It was early afternoon and both parents were at work. I opened the door to find two men in suits. "Are you James Wright?" Jesus, I thought, not again. "Mr. Wright, you're under arrest for failure to report for induction into the United States Army."

I had no idea how they found me. Maybe someone had seen me around town, someone who knew my fugitive status and didn't like it, or maybe the wiretap paid off. I never figured it out. Perhaps it was inevitable. The feds let me write a note, then it was the handcuffs and the back of their unmarked cruiser and a two-hour drive to Spokane. They booked me into the federal holding facility pending arraignment. Situated on an upper floor of the federal building in the center of the city, it wasn't a large jail. There were less than a dozen inmates, all of them bank robbers, except for one other guy picked up on a draft violation. The facility was clean and well-kept and after some of my previous incarcerations, it seemed bland.

I paid close attention to the bank robbers, who fascinated me. Avid card players, they were friendly and competed with each other in good-natured bragging about their exploits. I felt safe with these guys. They were the gentlemen of the blue-collar criminal set. Most of them seemed educated, intelligent, and articulate. As they told their stories, I saw the pattern: they'd knock off a bank for a few thousand, go on a spending spree, get busted, get a ten-year sentence, do the time, earn a few years off for good behavior, and as soon as they were released, they'd start planning the next bank robbery. Sometimes they got away with it, but they'd keep knocking over banks until they got busted. It's almost like they were compelled to rob banks and do time. I thought they worked it as a game, give and take, just a natural cycle of life. Even though guns featured in their crimes, they didn't want to shoot anybody; they didn't believe in violence. What they believed in was free money and the spree.

I was arraigned but deemed a flight risk, so no bail. I'd have to remain in custody until the trial. The other criminals in the federal unit had been there for months, so I gave up any hope of getting out soon. My prospects for trial weren't so hot, either. Though given a choice between jungle combat or prison, I'd already decided on the latter. The judge assigned me a public defender, just to keep everything legal.

I got lucky again, because the public defender turned out to be an experienced trial lawyer, one of the best in the city, picking up some pro bono work as part of his ethical obligation. We met in a small visitation room in the jail. A plump, well-dressed man, the lawyer exuded confidence. Not only that, but a sense of humor. He listened to me for a while, looked thoughtful, and announced, "So, you don't want to go into the Army." I owned that I did not. "Can't say as I blame you," he said. He asked me what I was doing to stay amused in jail and I told him I'd found an unabridged copy of *Don Quixote* in the prisoner library. That launched a quick exchange of literary preferences and I found out that we'd read and appreciated some of the same things. It looked like I'd gained not only a lawyer but an ally.

He asked me what I'd been doing while I wasn't in the Army and I told him about climbing and rambling in the mountains, riding freight trains, hitching, traveling the West, the drugs, my erratic efforts at writing, and pretty much everything there was to tell that wasn't too horrible. He didn't freak out or express judgment about any of it. He just smiled and asked more questions. After half an hour of this, he summed up his thoughts. "First, we're going to get you out of here. I've got an idea about that but you're going to have to promise me not to run." I nodded. "Secondly, I'll set up a meeting with a psychologist I know. He'll do a full, detailed assessment. You'll tell him everything you've told me and answer all his questions. I'm certain he's going to say you're not Army material. You understand me?"

I did. He was charting a way for me to be declared 4-F, unsuitable for military service. I couldn't believe it. If this worked, I wouldn't have to run another step.

I spent three more weeks in the federal cell, enough time to finish *Don Quixote*, which I enjoyed. After that, I started churning through Louis L'Amour Westerns, which made up most of the prison library. One of these books could be read in a couple of hours, hardly sufficient for getting through a day of incarceration. Not only that, each one was exactly like the others, and they were all dumb.

When I got bailed out, I was glad to see the open sky. Somehow, the lawyer had convinced the judge to let me go home to my parents' house on the condition that I stay there and report for trial. My Dad drove to Spokane to pick me up and on the ride home, he confided that they had used their house as collateral. I could tell he wasn't happy about it. I didn't blame him; I felt terrible. Given the circumstances, there was no way I could run off and forfeit my parents' home. I had to trust the lawyer's plan.

In a couple of weeks, I went back to Spokane and saw the psychologist. I wore my mountain clothes: anorak, an old, torn sweater, wool climbing knickers, ice climbing boots, the whole absurd costume. I wanted to represent the high-altitude desolation of my psyche, and I thought I should dress the part. None of these clothes had been washed in a while, so they carried an air of authenticity.

The psychologist was a nice man, dressed in a suit and tie, who sat behind a desk, asked questions, and took notes. The session lasted four hours. By the end, I had related the entire autobiography of my deeds and thoughts. I said stuff I'd never said to anyone. At the end, he said the same thing as my lawyer, "One thing is clear; you don't want to go into the Army, do you?" He was right about that. We shook hands and I caught the bus back home.

About two weeks later, my lawyer wanted to meet; he didn't say why, just that it was important. After another bus ride to Spokane, I sat in his office and read the psychologist's report while my lawyer shuffled papers on his desk. It was five pages of dense, single-spaced typescript, precise and faithful to our conversation. In fact, he captured me down to the soul. At the end, I read and re-read the last line: "Mr. Wright is unsuitable for military, industrial, or social adaptability." I almost choked. Was I that bad, that much of a freak? Maybe so.

"If you're willing to submit to another induction physical," the lawyer said, "the prosecutor will drop the charges. I recommend it. With this evaluation, there is no way they will take you."

It wasn't long before I received the induction notice; despite all the complaints about the sluggish pace of government bureaucracy, they never seemed to delay a chance to induct someone into the Army. I was nervous about the procedure, but the lawyer had been right with everything else, so I wanted to trust him. Besides, my parents' house was still on the line.

For a change, I went to the induction sober, clutching the envelope with the psychology assessment. I sailed through all the exam steps, the eye test, the fingers poking my balls and cough test, the blood pressure test, all the basic elements used by medical science to determine if someone is alive. I kept hoping they'd fail me for something, like my flat feet, but nothing was bad enough to disqualify me as a suitable opponent for the Viet Cong.

The last stage of the induction physical was a meeting with the Army psychiatrist. I handed him the envelope. He motioned me to sit down while he read the report. He read it quickly, which worried me. Was he absorbing the message or was he skimming it prior to dismissing it as inconsequential? He got to the last line and folded it up. After signing and stamping my induction form, he offered it to me along with the report, waving his hand that I should leave. He didn't say a word. Leaving meant that

I was not being drafted. Otherwise, it would have been straight out the big door and into a bus headed to boot camp. I looked at the induction form as I turned to leave. "4-F," it said, in red ink. I was free.

On the Greyhound home, I considered how to celebrate. Should I get drunk, or high, or just eat a whole chocolate cake? By the time I got off the bus, I'd given up on the celebration idea. What was I celebrating, anyway? Being a social and industrial zero? Being, in the eyes of science and the government, a useless entity? It seemed problematic to wallow in this. I was just glad to stop looking over my shoulder. A level of relaxation crept into my bones. A big obstacle had been removed. My future wasn't at all clear to me, but at least I knew it didn't involve death in the desperate jungle.

11

The Gorge of Despair

[a] Despite the perils of youth, I made it to twenty-two. That's when I met Andy and George in Yosemite Valley. They'd just completed an ascent of the Salathe Wall on El Capitan, one of the greatest rock climbs in the world. It took them four days, sleeping on minuscule ledges and grappling from dawn to dusk with the complex challenges presented by three thousand feet of vertical granite. The aesthetics and exposure of this climb made it one of the most desirable accomplishments on a rock climber's resume. By completing the Salathe, Andy and George secured their places among the young lions of the Valley.

I was more of a snake than a lion, sloughing skin for skin, always trying to be somebody else. I had done some short climbs around the Valley, including a few along the base of El Cap, undemanding routes of a pitch or two that stopped at a ledge where I could pretend to have surmounted something while the vast bulk of the cliff loomed overhead in silent admonishment. But you didn't have to be a great climber to live the life. It offered a lure for those of us dedicated to staying outside the norm and fascinated with trying on the costumes of the deviant. And after the crazy years of maximum drug use on the dirty, wet streets of Seattle, climbing seemed like a ray of light. I clung to its bright promise. It didn't hurt that it was a macho pursuit, and I was hungry to resolve many lingering questions about manhood. I tended to exaggerate my achievements as a cover for deep-seated insecurities. Or worse than stretching the truth, I allowed others to assume my accomplishments were greater than they were and then simply failed to enlighten them otherwise. I faked it, for the most part, because I wanted to be something. I wasn't sure what, but there was nothing new with that.

Andy and George, though, they were focused. Barely twenty years old, they were symbiotic climbing partners with serious ambitions. A dynamic duo, a self-contained unit, yet open to the world, friendly and gregarious, even to a duffer like me. That's the way it was in those days—you'd meet someone in camp, they'd say something clever or relatively sane, you'd feel a spark of connection, and the next day they'd have your life in their hands at the other end of a rope. Trust was often extended, unearned, and only withdrawn if abused.

I encountered Andy over a game of chess. It was the year that Fischer and Spassky played for the world championship, and enthusiasm ran high. The match ignited interest throughout America and people who had never thought about the game were playing or talking about it. For others, chess goes deeper and becomes an addictive and unforgiving master. To play at an expert level requires sacrifice. As Vladimir Nabokov observed, there is a continuum of players, from those who play "brief, uncomplicated games, remarkable neither for ambition nor inspiration" all the way up to the compulsively afflicted, for whom playing is like "performing a sacred rite." I lusted after the special cachet of the afflicted, as in everything else I'd done up to that point in life. I wanted to be focused and successful, an esoteric master of depth and mystery. However, I was anxious, easily distracted, and fundamentally undisciplined, not well suited for the rigors of sacred rites.

By the time Andy and I sat down in Yosemite to play chess, I'd been obsessed with the game for years. Or it might be more accurate to say that I was obsessed with the notion of being obsessed, a kind of pretension toward devotion that didn't require as much work or aptitude. During the depths of this phase I lived a solitary existence at a remote farmhouse in the woods of northeastern Washington. Since there were few visitors, I spent most of the daylight hours studying strategy books, pouring over variations in *Modern Chess Openings* (the closest thing to a chess-player's bible), replaying games of the grandmasters, working through the pros and cons of black-and-white options, and generally wasting my time. All this study made me a better-than-average player, but hardly one of note. I never tested myself, anyway, preferring to leave my fantasies unblemished. Besides, I smoked a lot of weed during my chess studies and retention was unpredictable.

In the fashion of American national parks, Yosemite offered more than natural amenities, including a village of consumer opportunities, an elite hotel with a lounge and expensive restaurant, numerous souvenir shops, and the proletarian Mountain Bar, an after-hours hangout for climbers who could afford the price of a drink. Chess was a diversion in the bar along with more conventional boozing activities, most of which involved shouting. You could sit in the aroma of smoke and sweat and listen to the heroes boast of their hard-earned scars. They were happy to muster an audience while they swilled beers and fulfilled the criteria of "the hard man," the British ideal of the degenerate stone master who leads a dissipated life while knocking off routes that no one else could even start.

I rarely had money to spend in the bar, but a few comrades urged me to check out the chess scene. I repressed my shyness and finally walked in, scanning the crowded tables for games in progress. There were two. I sauntered over to each table and stood for a while, silent and studious. With a casual pretense, I monitored both games and when one ended, I cleared my throat and addressed the winner, flush from his victory: "Hey. Want to play another?" And I was in for the duration. A couple nights of this and my face became linked with chess. I started going to the bar every day.

Chess brought me into contact with climbers of international reputation; some were legendary. An odd juxtaposition for me because, by comparison, even in my dreams I couldn't match up with these folks on the rock. But I could, and did, beat them at chess. This intrigued the hard men, at least enough to buy some brews and engage a duel. Like chess, rock climbing is an analytical pursuit. Both activities require imagination; you have to visualize the moves in advance and plan exactly what you're going to do. An aptitude for this is crucial for success in either endeavor. But just as playing chess won't get you five feet up a rock face, climbing is no preparation for the gymnastics of the chessboard. In the difference, I found a chance to mystify and cultivate some respect. I explained strategy to my opponents if they wanted to learn. Some did and were eager to test themselves again and again. In turn, I was happy to get free beer and hold my own with the heroes of the Valley.

I also played on the picnic tables of Camp 4, the climbers' camp, and when Andy saw me there, he immediately wanted a game. While we leaned over the board, we talked and found a liking for each other. Andy was charismatic, one of those larger-than-life people, a golden personality, full of laughter and infectious moods, a big, powerful young man who inspired friendship and affection in all who met him. He embodied the external qualities of a radiant Apollo that I craved for myself. But there was a dark side to him as well, bubbling with impatience, frustration, and an excess of nervous energy. It was his dark side that connected to my own and supplied us a language in common, a language whose symmetry carried the seeds of inevitable argument.

Andy's approach to chess was like his character: swashbuckling, risky, full of gusto and willing to offer a gambit if he thought it might activate a winning combination. My response to Andy's aggressive style was the same as it was for everyone who stormed across the board in a shower of pieces: I played a slow, congested game, declining exchanges or small sacrifices in order to keep the board cluttered and dense. This style requires tight maneuvers and devotion to a plan. A free-wheeling opponent gets frustrated with the suffocating position, thrashes around like a trapped animal, then makes a mistake. Once the mistake is made, it's only a matter of time before I grind home the advantage. Chess isn't a nice game. It breeds disdain, ego, greed, and a lust for power. I always wanted the win and I'd go all out to get it.

It didn't matter that much for Andy or any of the other climbers I played who won these games—they were friendly contests, diversions from the rock. The highest priority for climbers remained success on the walls; the rest of life could be a disaster. Many climbers came to Yosemite and stayed for months, primarily in the spring and fall when the weather was tolerable. If you wanted to be better, there was only one way to achieve that goal: climb as much as possible. Holding down a regular job was rare amongst the afflicted. At best, they would pick up seasonal work or get an unskilled job, labor for a few weeks or months, then quit when it was time to go climbing. A monkish life, though the name given to those who chose this lifestyle was more profane than sacred: dirtbags.

By this point, being a bum utilized a skill set I had honed to a habit. I lived outdoors in Camp 4 with the other dirtbags; you didn't even need a tent; a sheet of plastic would do. Food was free by scrounging the leftovers at the cafeteria, enabled by the summer Park workers. They didn't care that we snuck into the employee dorm showers for the occasional hygiene break. I carried my belongings in a backpack, hitchhiked around or rode freight trains, and avoided the entanglements of material and social obligations. The military wanted to send me to Vietnam, but they had to find me first. I didn't see the sense of a job; it would lead the feds straight to me. Nomadic instability was my survival strategy.

However, a little cash never hurt, so I sold marijuana. Friends from Seattle, enterprising dealers, were always interested in expansion opportunities, and both climbers and park employees had a fondness for marijuana. Every now and then, a dealer would drive into the park with bags of weed and front them to me and others they knew. The dope was so easy to sell it was criminal. I felt an uncouth pride in being the drug connection for some of the most famous climbers in the world, people who would show up in the magazines as the new hard men, pushing the standards. "Yeah, I sold dope to him. And him." But like a priest after confession, I couldn't say anything, not if I wanted to keep my customers.

Andy, though, liked to brag about introducing Joe Brown to weed. This was his favorite contribution to the evening storytelling in Camp 4. We'd sit around the picnic table in the dark and polish the mythology of deeds, embellishing the old stories anew, an essential contribution to the renegade climbing culture. Wherever climbers gathered, such recitation fed the hard man motif, shaping it into an archetype of aspiration for young climbers. The Brits were the champions of such gab, especially the boasting; not only did they invent the sport, they also determined the discourse. When the Manchester climber Joe Brown came to Yosemite, people took notice. He was a legend, the greatest of his generation, the original man of grit. Like the other Brits, he drank—a lot. They were a rowdy bunch, and they were not hippies. California, florid with psychedelic culture, came as a shock to them, including Joe Brown. One of the first people he ran into was Andy, who promptly convinced him to smoke a joint. Andy was like that; he could charm anyone into anything. Brown, of course, fell into uncontrollable giggles, revealing himself as mortal after all. Somehow, this felt like a victory, and we celebrated the tale through its many tellings.

Meeting Andy led me directly to George, his best friend and climbing partner. George was another radiant god, not so much an Apollo as a clever Hermes, eyes beaming through round spectacles and head topped with wild, bushy hair. As I soon learned, he was less mercurial than Andy, and I came to appreciate his steady, intelligent humor. George was strong like no one else I'd met. He could do one arm pull-ups and other gymnastic feats that seemed impossible to me. George attributed his strength and overall robust physique to his mother, who lived on a small organic farm in Oregon. She raised all her own food and specialized in meat, especially beef and pork. George claimed that every meal at his mother's, three times a day, featured big slabs of beef, bacon, and whatever else had been crammed into the freezer. He described the portions as fit for a predator. George thought it was too much; he wanted fruits and vegetables. In Yosemite, I never saw him take a bite of meat; he just ate bowls heaped with granola, yogurt, and fruit.

George wasn't into chess, but we shared other interests, especially literature. Talking about books was second nature for me, and we discussed everything we'd read and liked. His ideas of humor meshed well, too, ranging from subtle absurdity to goofy slapstick. George could be quite silly, a trait I shared, and we found each other hilarious. His essential optimism undermined my morbid tendencies, and I instinctively sought his company, even if I didn't recognize why. This made him an invaluable friend. I'm not sure what I provided in exchange. I could make him laugh, which was a reward in itself, and maybe that's enough for friendship.

[b]   After climbing the Salathe Wall, Andy and George were hungry for a new challenge. Somehow, we'd become a trio, despite my mediocre climbing skills, and we idled together in Camp 4, thumbing through old climbing magazines, and indulging ourselves with wild talk. Even though Yosemite was the best place in the world for rock climbing, once you got there it was fashionable to act bored and claim that you'd rather be somewhere else, somewhere even more fabulous. Of course, everyone wanted to find a hidden Yosemite, to be the first to lay hands on new rock. Andy perked up when I shared an article from the *American Alpine Journal* about a small expedition to a remote valley in King's Canyon National Park, a hundred miles south of Yosemite.

"Check this out." I pointed to a photo of a particularly sick-looking rock formation.

"What the hell is that?"

"Tehipite Dome. Down in King's Canyon, smack dab in the middle of fucking nowhere. Climbed once. From the back. The face is untouched."

"Whaaa?"

"You heard me. And surrounded by unnamed, unclimbed stuff. Lots of stuff."

"Shit, when do we leave?"

Having a bookish inclination, I loved research; I could spend hours digging in journals and beetling my way across maps. I was a better researcher than climber; pouring over two-dimensional data seemed so much easier than the hard work of climbing in three. George and Andy appreciated my knack because wilderness exploration requires research if you don't want to waste time and energy. They liked what I dredged up from the archives. Finding new areas, of course, was only a prelude to putting up new routes. Earning a first ascent was like receiving a golden apple and everybody wanted them. You'd get your name in the guidebook, a kind of immortality. The champion of first ascents was Fred Beckey from Washington, who would climb anything if he could claim a first. His obsession was downright manic. Skeptics noted that many of his routes were on crumbling rock, overgrown with vegetation, difficult to get to, unappealing in almost every way. No one wanted to deal with crap like that, even for a first ascent. But it didn't stop Beckey. His lifestyle was completely oriented to climbing new routes, nothing else mattered. As a result of this focus, he had so many firsts—reportedly more than a thousand in North America alone—that even Fred didn't know for sure how many he had done.

And the article that captured our attention was written by Fred Beckey himself. Almost a decade earlier, his party of four achieved the first ascent of Tehipite Dome. Even if they had avoided the gigantic 3600-foot wall rising out of the valley, the expedition sounded epic. His descriptions of the arduous 21-mile hike to the dome lugging monster loads of climbing equipment was intimidating enough, but when he described the challenge of crossing the raging torrents in the valley, we were intimidated. For Beckey and his team, following the trail to the base of the dome would have required them to ford Crown Creek, a minor tributary of the Middle Fork of the King's River.

It was in full flood and was so daunting to them that they elected to re-shoulder their loads and hike back out of the valley, circling the dome from the high country and accessing a shorter way to the summit. He argued against the need to "fight a torrent, yucca plants, and rattlesnakes" just to bag the summit, even if that meant skipping the iconic wall towering above the valley. Beckey was notorious for bushwhacking through anything to get to a climb, so if it was too much for him, we didn't want to touch it. As far as we knew, the vast wall remained unclimbed, along with all the other potential routes along the cliffs bordering the valley. From the article alone, Andy, George, and I convinced ourselves that Tehipite Valley was a new Yosemite. Even Beckey suggested it. We couldn't understand why no one had followed him to this astounding temple of granite. In time, somebody would, and that might as well be us.

Although Tehipite Dome was clearly a prize, we couldn't stop thinking about an area on the other side of the river, opposite the dome, a tributary gorge drawn on the map with intense topographic lines, lines so tightly spaced you could practically see the vertical walls. The Gorge of Despair, it was named, one of those gruesome labels that sound dire to the masses and make climbers' hearts beat faster. The mythology of death and darkness is a mainstay in mountain nomenclature, producing places like Devil's Thumb, Forbidden Peak, Death Bivouac, Mt. Terror, Highway to Hell, The Ogre, and The Worst Error. Something about the mountains brings out the morbid. Most climbers don't have death wishes, but they appreciate that the proximity of death intensifies the life force in each crazy moment. The threat of termination catalyzes an adrenaline-fueled rush of vitality, a powerful and addictive high. Each climb carries the potential of meeting the Grim Reaper and when climbers die in action, they are said to be "chopped," as if cut down with the scythe. You accept it or you don't climb. Instead of summoning a cloud of depression, the so-called Gorge of Despair stoked our excitement, luring us onward with the tease of looking into nature's stony face and seizing some glory.

Consumed with the challenge of the gorge, we did more research and learned that the Middle Fork of the King's River had never been forded in spring; it was too deep, too fast, and too treacherous. As hard as it was to get to Tehipite Dome, it was going to be even harder to get to the Gorge of Despair. The only trail into Tehipite Valley wouldn't do, not for the gorge; we needed an alternate route, one that didn't involve crossing the river.

"Nobody wants to mess with that current. Especially not at high water, like spring, like now!" George tried to sound a precautionary note, but his voice cracked with excitement. Everything about this trip promised adventure.

"Hell no, me included. I'm not swimming any rivers." Andy paced back and forth as George and I leaned over the map on the picnic table.

I stabbed my finger onto a place marked Cedar Grove. "Look. If we pick up the trail out of here, it links to this trail and then this trail and in about a dozen miles we climb up to Happy Gap at 9000 feet. From there it's cross-country, no trail, but downhill, or on the contour. We truck along the Silver Creek drainage, pop over this little ridge, then down to Tehipite Valley. On the south side of the river, where we want to be. No need to get wet."

The Silver Creek route looked complicated but far from impossible. By this time, I had a couple years of experience route finding and battling brush in the North Cascades, mountains with notorious off-trail difficulties. Hardly a comprehensive resume but enough to muster a credential of sorts. George and Andy claimed to have spent little time off-trail, and they were happy to concede the scouting to someone who had survived devil's club, impenetrable alder thickets, and the labyrinthine confusions of the wild, old-growth forests of the Northwest. Most climbers would rather deal with a thousand feet of vertical rock than a hundred feet of undergrowth. So, they took my advice. But it didn't take a master explorer to see that there weren't a lot of options: if we wanted to end up on the south side of the river with access to the Gorge of Despair this was the route. The alternatives were worse, much worse.

[c] It was May, a beautiful month in the Sierras, and it was only going to get hotter and drier. We saw no reason to delay. We used Andy's money to buy a heap of provisions, enough to stay for weeks in paradise. We sorted gear and loaded up our packs. With food, climbing apparatus, and camping equipment they were 80 pounds each. There's nothing enjoyable about humping such a load, but that's the price of admission. We could have trimmed the weight by taking less climbing gear or less food, but then we'd be shortchanging our adventure. We wanted to climb new routes in a wild place, little known, rarely tasted, and all ours. For that, we would carry the burdens.

None of us had a car, but my friend Drone—fresh in from New Mexico—had a Willys 4x4 station wagon, and he agreed to drive us to King's Canyon and drop us at the trailhead. We didn't have a plan for the return. We talked vaguely about hitchhiking back to the Valley, sometimes trailing off into "maybe we'll just stay there...."

The drive took most of the day, west from Yosemite, south to Fresno on 99, then east back into the Sierras. Once we entered Kings Canyon National Park, we stopped to walk through the sequoia trees in the Grant Grove. The trees were so big that it was impossible to consider our aspirations as anything other than trivial under the aloof splendor of those giants, the largest trees on earth. At first, we babbled with excitement, then grew silent as we wandered through the grove. Language simply couldn't encompass the scale.

Humbled, we crawled back into the car for the last leg to Cedar Grove. There we found another national park consumer interface with services to appeal to the auto-bound tourist. We weren't interested. As soon as we found the trail, we'd be self-sufficient, released from civilization and free in our own realm. At the trailhead, we smoked a joint with Drone, said good-bye, shouldered the loads, and marched into the arid woods. We walked a couple of miles and camped for the night, primed to make Tehipite in a one-day push.

The next day, we started fresh, buoyant, settling into the loads, fiddling with the adjustments on our packs, seeking the zone of least effort. About an hour into it we'd downshifted to the lowest gear, put one foot in front of the other, and donned the beast-of-burden consciousness. The packs were heavy and impossible to ignore, but the trail walking was uncomplicated.

We distracted ourselves with daydreams and occasional chatter. It was work, but nothing we couldn't do.

In the Sierra Nevada, most of the surface water comes from melting snow; by the end of spring, snow only remains at the highest elevations. It's a dry range. Rain is rare and temperatures can soar, parching all life except for that with the deepest roots. Summer wasn't far away, and as we labored along the trail, we wondered what climbing might be like in Tehipite on the scorching hot granite. Any labor, though, seemed alluring if it didn't involve backpacking. Meanwhile, there was nothing to do but grunt, drink water, and carry on.

The trail ended at Happy Gap as we crested the ridge where we could look down into the headwater basin of Silver Creek. It was not a happy place for us; we stepped off the trail and into a chest-high maze of manzanita. A beautiful chaparral bush, perfect for landscaping, manzanita features bright green leaves and gnarly growths of red branches. Unfortunately for the wilderness traveler, the branches are tough and stiff and form nearly impenetrable thickets. At Happy Gap we gazed across masses of manzanita covering the ground in all directions. Being able to see over the brush made it seem inconsequential at first, but as we tried to push through it, we found that making progress required the power of a bull. We threw ourselves at it again and again, battering ahead as the rough branches tore at our efforts, slicing and scraping any available flesh. All remnants of good mood evaporated in the heat and toil. Looking ahead, we saw a mile or more of manzanita that would have to be traversed to follow the contours down and around the head of the drainage.

We needed to descend from Happy Gap at 9600 feet to Tehipite Valley at 5000 while covering about three or four linear miles. Without a trail, our best strategy took the line of least resistance. The tight, squiggly lines on the topo map advertised what was near the bottom of the Silver Creek drainage: steep walls. We planned to stay as high above these walls as possible until we could slip through an unnamed gap over the north ridge. From this gap, it looked like we could scramble all the way down into Tehipite Valley. Modern topo maps provide the information to interpret contours and how to navigate terrain, even if you've never been there. Of course, there are things they don't show, like the difference between forest and brush; it's all shaded the same hue of green. At the upper end of the Silver Creek drainage the contours are relatively gentle, which would have made them simple to negotiate except for the manzanita. According to the map, traversing high around the headwater basin would eventually lead us to steep terrain. On the map, that was all green, but we could see from the pass that the manzanita changed to forest, and no matter how steep, that seemed feasible for travel. It was the lower part of the drainage that I wanted to avoid, especially down toward the mouth where it twisted into a bottleneck gorge of vertical rock. The map made it look daunting, if not impossible. By staying high in the forest, we hoped we could maintain the contour all the way to the gap in the ridge. We'd spent hours studying the map; it didn't look easy, but it should go.

After hours of thrashing, we emerged, exhausted, from the manzanita. Our moods were foul, and we hated the packs; they were ridiculous. We groused about bringing so much stuff, even if it seemed essential at the time. We were thirsty and hot and getting low on water. We had last refilled from a feeder stream that cascaded through the manzanita, but we'd already consumed most of that. We drank the rest in celebration of our escape from the brush, leaving a few token swallows just in case. Shouldering our loads, we headed on, into the upper reaches of the forest. The map suggested we might cross another feeder stream or two, although when we got to them, they were dry. At least the trees gave shade, a respite from the baking sun.

Our relief was short-lived because, just like the map predicted, the slope steepened as we left the basin. Before long we were walking sidehill on precarious terrain. Even though we were under trees, they were widely spaced, and a fall would be difficult to arrest until you slammed into a trunk, preferably sooner than later. The dense soil made for tough going; hard to call it walking. You had to step precisely from foot to foot, forcing the edge of your boot into the slope. Nowhere could you place the sole flat on the ground. Doing this with an eighty-pound pack was like trying to dance with a pig on your shoulders. If we had thought the manzanita was torment, this was another circle of hell.

Well short of our objective for the day, the sun dropped out of the sky. We had to make camp, somehow. There was no place to pitch a tent or even set the packs without risking them rolling down the hill. Our only hope lay in clinging to the trees. We each chose a tree where the accumulated soil on the uphill side provided enough level ground to lay a sleeping bag. There wasn't enough room in these spots to stretch out, but at least the tree would hold us against the slope and block us from a helpless descent during the night. We might have laughed at having to do a cliff-type bivouac in the woods, but it didn't seem funny, not in the slightest.

We were too tired to complain. In one day, we had devolved from aspiring wilderness heroes to beaten souls. Cooking a meal could restore some of our spunk, but we didn't have enough water. The nearest water lay two or three thousand feet straight down the hill in the bowels of Silver Creek. We thought about the effort required to go and haul it back. Suddenly, Andy said, "Fuck it, I'm going." Before George or I could object, he grabbed two water jugs and disappeared down the hill. We looked at each other in disbelief but with a sprinkle of hope. We pulled out the white-gas stove, a pot, and the dried makings of a stew, combining our last remaining water.

It was pitch dark before Andy returned with two full jugs. He collapsed on the perch next to us, unable to say more than "Fuckin' long way...." He didn't need to elaborate; in the dim light of the stove, his face said enough. We sat close together and ate our portions of the stew, too tired for conversation. With nothing left to do, we retired to the tiny perches at our individual trees and cautiously crawled into our sleeping bags.

[d]   It was an awful night. The smooth nylon of our sleeping bags provided a slippery confinement. I was sure that at any moment I would slide off my pad and plunge into the darkness, thrashing helplessly as I rolled, trapped in my cocoon. The uphill side of the tree offered two or maybe three-square feet of flat ground, then it angled around the trunk. We curled into awkward balls to stay on the flat part. Stretching out required letting the head or feet, or a little of each, hang along the inclines. After

hours of experimental postures, I settled on occupying the flat part from head to hips, dangling my legs down the hill, hoping that I'd mustered enough body mass for a stable anchor. It was a delicate balance and minor shifts of position emphasized the threat of gravity. And the slick nylon only enhanced that threat. I slept in fits. Periodically, I heard muttered cursing from the other two as they tried to adapt to their perches.

We were awake when the first light of dawn slipped into the woods. Crawling out of our bags, we packed them away before eating a meal of granola and milk. Thanks to Andy's sacrifice the night before, we had plenty of water to mix with the milk powder. As we shoveled down the glop, we discussed our itinerary.

"If we stay on this contour, we'll get to the saddle and can work our way down to Little Tehipite Valley. Sucks, but it'll go." I tried to be optimistic. Little Tehipite was a small wide spot on the Middle Fork a few miles downstream from the Gorge of Despair. We didn't know what travel along the river would be like, but having a wide spot next to the river, even a small wide spot, was alluring. George nodded his head in agreement as he ate his cereal.

Andy's face, however, was taut with fatigue and anger. "Fuck this shit! Fuck it! Let's go down Silver Creek. How bad can it be?"

I stared at him in shock. "Hell, man, look at those damn cliffs downstream! We can't lug these packs through that!"

Andy's look was a pure dagger, and he sliced his words with precision. "You... don't... know. I'd rather deal with rock than more of this stupid slope."

"No, man, no, we need to stay up here and keep at it. Going down there is nuts!"

Andy clenched his jaw so hard I thought he would crush his own teeth: "You didn't see it; I did. I say we can do it."

Andy and I were swallowed by the barely repressed fury of the argument. George tried to interject some calm, using an even voice as he strained to rekindle our usual good humor. But his perspective agreed with mine, and the peacemaking only irritated Andy. I pushed hard to stay with the plan. It was tightly reasoned, the result of careful map study. I was invested in it, like the strategy for a chess match. True, I was being rigid, dense, caught up in my own complications. Andy felt suffocated. He wanted the breakout combination, the key that unlocked the winning line. His comfort with the technical challenges of rock left him preferring open slopes of granite over the humiliation of dirt hills, buried in shade. He made his points, but I couldn't dismiss my fear of the unknown hazards that lurked in the depths of Silver Creek. We argued around in circles for a while, then Andy, the man of action, came to his decision. "I'm going down. If you guys want to stay up high, then stay up high. But I'm going down."

George and I were aghast. At first, we didn't know what to say. It was unthinkable, a mutiny. "We can't split up, that's the worst! No!"

Andy was adamant: "Then come with me."

"You've got to be kidding."

"Whatever. I'm going down."

George radiated distress at the prospect of separating from his friend. I felt it, too. But climbers are individualistic, opinionated, and headstrong, as committed as chess fanatics to the passion of their endeavors. Criticism doesn't count for much. For those who aim beyond the norm, this is a common, perhaps necessary flaw.

Andy wasn't swayed by our pleas, although we begged him to reconsider. The discussion was over; he was going down. None of us liked it, but we couldn't break through the stalemate. So, we made a new plan. Andy would make a solo descent of Silver Creek, meeting the Middle Fork of the King's River at Little Tehipite Valley. George and I would continue along our contour to the saddle, go over the ridge and down through the woods to the river, which would put us at the upper end of Little Tehipite. Whoever got to Little Tehipite first would set up camp in an obvious spot and then wait for the other party. A terrible plan, but we agreed on it.

I said no more, but I was dismayed. Splitting up seemed a foolish risk. We had food, water, gear, and our health. It was just a matter of laboring on, and we'd get there. Andy didn't see it that way. He was pissed off and refused to submit to a majority. I sympathized with his frustration, but not the rash improvisation. George didn't like it, either. We could have followed him down, but by that time we were pissed off, too. Fuck him. Silver Creek had stripped away the glamour of our adventure, leaving us exposed in stubborn pride. Oh well, we'd beat him to Little Tehipite and tease him when he got there.

Andy hiked down through the trees into the unknown entrails of Silver Creek. George and I watched him go, saying nothing. He didn't look back and when he disappeared, we hoisted our packs and trudged off across the slope. Andy was right about one thing; our route was slow and taxing. The slope remained unforgiving, and a stumble would be dangerous. We treaded with caution, trying to avoid any loss of elevation. It's always tempting to take the next step slightly downhill because it's just a bit easier. We fought that urge, forcing ourselves to push up the slope to stay on the contour, walking in deliberation, letting our focus on the task stifle the need to talk about what happened.

After only two or three hours of sidehill tedium we found ourselves at the saddle in the ridge. From there, the valley of the Middle Fork stretched out below us. Upstream loomed the massive wall and round cap of Tehipite Dome. It dominated the valley with granite majesty. Here we were, with our dreams at our feet. The route ahead looked uncomplicated. We looked at each other with the same thought: why the fuck didn't Andy stay with us?

We hiked down from the saddle with a little scrambling, but nothing difficult. By early afternoon we were in Little Tehipite Valley. A gentle breeze cooled the sweat from our skin as we meandered around giant pines along the bottom land bordering the river. Underfoot, the soft needles were a welcome carpet. It was a campsite in paradise. We checked on the map and saw that when Andy got to the river, as he turned and followed it upstream, he wouldn't miss the spot, so we pitched the tent and sat down to wait.

It was a glorious Sierra afternoon, warm and dry, a perfect day to sit in the shade and listen to the river pounding past the rocks. Here, the Middle Fork was about a hundred feet wide, slightly past full spring flood but still fast and deep. A crossing looked impossible and confirmed our expectation that we would not be visiting Tehipite Dome. The sight of the dome, however, had fired our expectations for the Gorge of Despair. So far, everything was bigger and even more spectacular than we had anticipated. George and I chattered away like squirrels, looking at maps, snacking, and guzzling the clear, chilled water of the river while we lounged against the tree trunks. We kept looking down the river for Andy, anxious to share the excitement. Any minute now we should see him toiling along, exhausted from his descent. We would brag about our route and snicker at his, but above all we would delight at being together again, finally where we wanted to be, ready to collect our treasure.

The day wore on without Andy. Eventually, the light began to wane, and worry became our preoccupation. Where the hell was he? We couldn't talk about it without the anxiety ripping through us like raw voltage, so we didn't. At twilight we fixed a tasteless dinner, eaten in silence and fear. It had only taken us half a day to get to Little Tehipite—he should have made it down long before dark. He should have. George and I crawled into the tent and had a fitful night. Surely by morning he would get to us.

We crawled out at the first hint of light. Still hoping to see him walking up the river at any moment, we fixed breakfast, enough for three. Glancing downstream every few minutes, we talked about possibilities. Andy could have run into obstacles and been forced to make camp; he might still be hiking toward us; in which case he would show up soon. A definite possibility. But there were other possibilities. An accident, for example. We didn't want to, but we talked about it. He could be hurt, unable to move, even a twisted ankle could prevent movement through this terrain. Andy was strong as an ox, but there's a limit to endurance and that limit comes sooner under heavy loads. A stumble at the wrong place, a loss of balance, a fall. Possible. Unseen among the rocks, a rattlesnake strike; he'd have no choice but to sit and sweat out the toxin. Whatever might have happened, he had food, water, clothes, a sleeping bag—enough to survive. He could be found and rescued. His sleeping bag was brilliant red; he could spread that on the ground, which would be easy to spot from the air. We didn't talk about death; there was no reason to talk about that.

With no other way to curb our mounting concerns, we hiked down the river to scout the mouth of Silver Creek, imagining that we would encounter Andy dragging along; we would laugh to see him and let our worries go. But there was nothing to see at Silver Creek, just a cascade of clear water racing out of the gorge. The creek bed was carved between steep granite walls, hundreds of feet high. We peered up the canyon, but it looked impenetrable. There was no shore, just a cold, sharp interface between rock walls and water.

George and I walked back to our camp overwhelmed with gloom. Optimism had been flushed away by the sight of the gorge. It was time to make a new plan. Like it or not, we had to think about a rescue.

[e]   We sat on a rock next to the river and stared at the rapids. My emotions tumbled around with the current, the same thoughts cresting over and over. Sorting anxiety from reality seemed impossible. Perhaps there would be no sorting; the situation was grim; worry was justified. Yet something had to be

done, didn't it? What, exactly? If Andy was dead, there would be no way to bring him back to life.

As I fretted, I felt George's solid presence next to me. I looked away from the churning river and into his face; his expression was carefully blank. Normally he would be smiling, taking a wry amusement in everything around him, or laughing so hard that his crown of bushy hair bobbed with a life of its own. Now, his eyes met mine and I saw determination. "Like it or not, we have to hike out of here. We need help."

"Should we give it more time? Another day? What if he shows up after we're gone? We've dumped the whole trip." I didn't say it, but I didn't want to deal with this. I wanted things to be the way they were.

"Andy's in trouble. I just feel it. We can't afford to waste time."

"Man, this is fucked up. Why did he go off like that? Fuck!" I wrestled with denial. A series of emotions wrinkled through George's face with variations of sympathy and grief before settling back into resignation.

"Come on. If he turns up okay, that's great. We'll all have a laugh. But if he needs help..."

"Yeah, you're right. Not much point in waiting any longer. He should be here by now. If we can get someone to fly over in a helicopter, they'd be able to spot him." Having avoided Vietnam so far, I didn't know if that was true—I had no idea how much you could see from a helicopter. Nor was I eager to find out. For a lark, my mother had bought me a ride on a Cessna two-seater at the county fair when I was ten years old, one of the most terrifying experiences of my life. But at this point it was easy to believe in the magic of machines and airborne technology. I needed to believe in something.

It didn't take long to devise a plan: hike out of the wilderness, contact the county sheriff, report the missing person, request aerial reconnaissance. If they couldn't find him then we'd know: he was chopped. Worse burial places could be found. For now, George and I would leave our tent where it was along with all the extra gear and a note in case Andy materialized out of Silver Creek. We'd carry day packs as light as possible, and we'd walk fast, driven by urgency.

The thought of going back the way we came, scrambling over the ridge, across the brutal side slopes, and uphill through the manzanita only to face miles of trail beyond that forced us to consider the alternative. Directly across the river was a maintained hiking trail that could lead us all the way out of the wilderness without the unpredictable obstacles of cross-country travel. True, it was over 20 miles of walking, but unburdened and at a brisk clip, we imagined covering that distance in a day. This seemed the most expedient way: we just had to get over the river. Never mind that it had a reputation for being impassable. We had to try for Andy's sake. If we couldn't make it, well, we'd have to go the other way.

Once decided, we set off upstream to scout a crossing. Our rucksacks each held a sleeping bag, water, and a little bit of food. As soon as we found the trail, we'd go full speed until dark, all the way to the road if possible. If not, we'd sleep under a tree and resume at daybreak. Simple enough, if the river didn't stop us. It seemed worth the gamble, cutting in half the time to initiate a rescue. That'd be one less day of Andy lying somewhere, fighting for his life, if that's what he was doing.

The map showed that two miles upstream the river cut a wide passage, forming the plain of Tehipite Valley. Where it was wider it would also be shallower, reducing the force of the current, perhaps yielding a ford. We scouted the shore as we walked, hoping for a gift from the gods, a tree fallen over the river, large enough to span the width and safe enough to walk above the torrent. There was nothing like that. We weren't surprised; we didn't believe in the gods. Even if a tree had fallen from shore to shore, it would likely have been ripped out in the spring flood and dragged down in the relentless migration to the sea.

As the valley widened, we caught glimpses of the rock formations flanking the Gorge of Despair. The walls were steep and intriguing. It was a beautiful place, Tehipite Valley, broad and flat, overseen by the commanding tower of Tehipite Dome looming from the other side of the river. We stared at the dome in awe, but there was no time to linger and gape. If there was going to be a way across the river, it would be here on the bottomland. The map depicted two channels through this section. We reasoned that each channel would be half the force of the full river. Scrambling along the gravel shore on the east side, we could see that the first course wasn't deep, maybe less than a foot. A rocky bottom, slippery and awkward for wading, but hardly a life-threatening challenge. We found stout branches of driftwood to use for staves, took off our boots and gingerly picked our way across the icy water. It was cold, but that was the worst of it. If the other crossing was like this, we would soon be on the trail.

The peak of spring flooding had passed and much of the river course was now dry, composed of stones, gravel, and a few hardy shrubs. We walked over the shifty rocks, a mix of large and small ball bearings—slow-going, ankle-bending terrain. The next branch of the river ran deeper, but we rejoiced to find a pine tree washed down, ripped out of the bank during a surge and lodged sideways across the channel. The massive root wad of the tree stood on the gravel bar and elevated most of the trunk over the current. We scrambled up the roots and onto the log. We wanted to prance across, nonchalant and in control, but once we stood on the trunk, it felt too narrow for that. Avoiding a plunge into the rocky stream seemed more than prudent, so we sat down, straddled it, and scooted across. Inglorious, but effective. At the other end of the tree, the top didn't quite make the far shore, so we had to lower ourselves into the water and wade the final bit. On dry land, we stopped, shook hands and congratulated ourselves, having mastered the fearsome Middle Fork. We did, for a moment, wonder how it had gotten its reputation.

We churned across the gravel, whooping and bragging about our feat, eager for the trail. We didn't get far before we could see there was more water ahead. The river wasn't finished with us, after all. So, there were three channels, not two. Whenever the map had been made, there had been two, but rivers change, especially in the flats. Now we were up against the real thing, the main branch of the river from the looks of it: wide and fast with standing whitecaps. Beyond the far bank the land started its rise toward the skirts of Tehipite Dome. The trail lay in the woods along that shore, a few yards from the river, if the map was to be believed. All we had to do was get across this third branch.

At this point there was no turning back; we were so close to the trail we could throw a rock and hit it. But there would be no tree bridges; this was a ford through violent water across slippery and shifting rocks. Waist-deep water is dangerous; if you lose your balance, the current will take you away, rolling you downstream until you're slammed against a rock. The year before, in the North Cascades, I got swept away by such a stream, completely helpless in the torrent as I bashed into boulder after boulder, finally thrown to the edge of the current as it tore around a bend, left to drag myself out of the water, bleeding and exhausted. All it takes is one misstep, one teeter, and you're gone. We had to try, but we had to escape the river unharmed. If we screwed up, we'd be the ones needing rescue.

For better footing, we kept our boots on. We still had the staves, which would be essential for the passage. We discussed the technique we'd use, planning our line of attack like we would a rock climb. Slow and steady, we'd push our way across the current, using the stick as a downstream prop for stability, moving it carefully from placement to placement, shifting with deliberate movements, and above all, sustaining balance at every point. One at a time, George first, we crossed the branch, taking an angle upstream so we could lean into the current, with less chance of being thrown off-kilter. This lengthened the crossing and stretched our endurance. Halfway through, the water came up to my waist and pushed with a terrible power. It took all my strength to keep moving. It would be so easy to just let go of the impossible labor and join the flow. But fear kicked in, and with it, adrenaline. I didn't want to die. Not here. I pushed on, a machine, and stopped thinking about how much longer I could hold out. There was only movement, one after another. And finally, a slackening of the current, the water grew shallower, and the rocks of the shore lay in front of me.

I emerged from the water to George's cheers, pleased at my success. We were soaked, but it didn't matter. We had crossed the mighty Middle Fork, once and for all.

It might have been a triumph of sorts, but in truth, it was nothing. We'd barely started; over twenty miles of trail remained, then we had to walk or hitchhike down roads to get to a telephone. Our goal was a camping village on Wishon Reservoir; we hoped to call the sheriff from there. After leaving our camp, it took several hours to cross the river and get to the trail; there wasn't much daylight left. Every moment seemed precious; in our minds, squandering time was squandering Andy's life, whatever was left of it. We hit the trail hard, setting off at a leg-stretching pace.

As soon as we started up the first, steep grade out of the valley, we had to go slower, even though we wanted to run. There was no sense in burning out in the first few miles. We ignored the viewpoints—no doubt entrancing—but we didn't even take a glance. We kept our heads down, focused on the trail, concentrating on each breath and each step.

The steepness of the trail eased off as we climbed out of the valley onto a vast tree-covered plateau. We gladly lengthened our stride, almost to a running gait, loping like wolves on the hunt. We tore through the meadows of Crown Valley, looking neither left nor right, just pushing on. The miles went by while the sun drained out of the sky. Soon it would be dark. We had no flashlight, no headlamp, nothing like that—a lesson to be filed away with the others. In the darkness, the trail would become hazardous; there were too many roots and rocks and even a sprained ankle would undermine Andy's rescue.

The last vestiges of light forced us to find someplace to sleep, on the ground, under a bush, somewhere. Suddenly, out of the gloom, we saw a ranger's shelter. It was a primitive cabin on the edge of a meadow, a place where trail crews might park their horses and set up a base for maintenance work. As usual with backcountry shelters, it was unlocked. I found a kerosene lamp and lit it. After tossing our sleeping bags on bunks, we ate some of George's gorp and discussed the next day. All we wanted was to report a missing person and ask for an aerial search. If Andy was alive, he knew enough to make himself visible. Once we filed our report, we figured that we would hike back in, gather our things and walk out, though we were unclear how any of this would proceed. It didn't seem to matter. Only Andy mattered.

[f]   Dawn's light poked into the cabin at an early hour, filtered and dispersed by the trees. I didn't know what time it was; neither of us wore a watch, a meaningless artifact in the wilderness. Sun was up; it was time to march.

We fueled ourselves with more gorp and hit the trail. It was relatively flat, and the map promised that it would stay like that until we started the descent from the high plateau to Wishon Reservoir. Relieved to have easy going, we flew over the ground in bounding strides. There was nothing left to think or talk about, only the mission, and that no longer required words, so we raced in a mindless state, attuned to the refinement of movement for maximum speed. Both miles and time slipped past. We saw no humans, no animals, and the forest seemed drained of life.

The sun still hadn't reached zenith when we raced out of the woods onto a dirt road. We had hoped to find a car at the trailhead with hikers who would agree to run us to the reservoir. But the parking area was deserted. We trooped off without pause, discussing the chances that someone might drive up this spur road, looking for the wilderness. No one came. We hadn't expected it, but we kept tormenting ourselves with hope, no matter how faint. Repeatedly, we looked over our shoulders or down the road for cars. We were so tired we couldn't help ourselves. It was a relief to finally drag our exhausted bodies around a corner and arrive at the Wishon concession store.

We barged through the door and blurted our predicament to the guy at the register. Without hesitation, he put the phone on the counter, pointing to a sign with local emergency numbers. George dialed the Fresno County sheriff's department. Suddenly I felt useless, an extraneous bit of matter wedged into a narrow segment of space, no reason for my existence. I wondered if George felt the same way. We had been so energized and focused on this one thing: get to a phone and make the call. Now it was done and, perhaps, so were we.

George hung up. "We're supposed to wait here. They're sending somebody to pick us up."

"For what?" I was still lost in space.

"Sounds like they're going to take us to the staging area for the rescue. They want us in." I saw that the prospect of action, of being able to do something for Andy, energized George. He was excited and ready for the next thing. As for me, I became anxious, wondering what it would mean to be "in." The storekeeper gave us each a soda, a small kindness that eased my nerves a little. George and I walked outside to wait.

About an hour later, a jeep sped up the road and braked to a hard stop in front of the store. The jeep was part of the sheriff's backcountry fleet, with a light bar, whipcord antenna, brush guard, and big tires. A uniformed deputy jumped out and introduced himself as Pete. We shook hands and he urged us to get in. He was stoked and primed for action. He seemed manic to me, but it was no time for doubts. George sat in the front seat, and I scrambled into the back. George started chatting and joking with Pete while I settled into the small jump seat.

"You'll want to buckle that seat belt." Pete provided this comment in a way that made it clear he meant it as more than a suggestion. He immediately stomped on the gas, and I fumbled to hook the belt as he roared away from the store, laying rubber, and tearing through the gears. Pete was obviously a lunatic and was going to get us killed. Had we survived fifty miles of wilderness travel only to die in a government machine? I managed to get strapped in, but I found myself tightening the seat belt repeatedly as we careened down the mountain. George, unfazed, gabbed with Pete while I locked my body to everything I could find, clenching grab bars and wedging my knees against the back of the driver's seat.

The road down from the reservoir was steep and winding. On the northern sides of slopes and in the heavier forest, we saw plenty of snow left from winter. Pete flew around the corners at full speed, lights flashing, ignoring any possibility of oncoming traffic, somehow satisfied with the knowledge that all obstacles would part for the sheriff's progress. I didn't share his confidence and clenched my jaw to avoid screaming at Pete to slow down. Finally, he rounded a corner too fast, and we slid off the road, airborne until we slammed into the snowpack like a rock into mud. I was glad for the seat belt. The jeep still ran, but it was buried to the tops of the wheels; despite Pete's attempts to gun it back and forth, it was stuck.

The rescue was shaping up to be another catastrophe. I didn't like cops anyway and this wasn't helping. I silently cursed Pete and his idiotic recklessness. But he was nonplussed. He jumped out of the jeep and surveyed the situation, closely followed by George and more reluctantly, me. Pete started to shovel out the tires while George and I collected small branches. The snowpack was several feet deep and though it was mostly firm, there were soft spots that resulted in sudden plunges into its icy grip as we tried to walk on it. We broke the branches into short sections and shoved them under the tires as a kind of makeshift platform to support the next attempt at extrication. Before we had a chance to test our efforts, another jeep came up the road and pulled over. Out hopped a jovial citizen who was pleased to be able to aid and assist law enforcement. He and Pete were instant chums. The citizen's jeep had a winch on the bumper, and it didn't take long before he positioned his jeep and cranked Pete's rig out of the snow. There were lots of hearty gestures and banter common to men at work, which George tried to join, somewhat lamely, I thought. I looked on, seething, full of intensity that couldn't be expressed.

Before long we were strapped in the jeep, zooming down the road. Pete apparently learned nothing from the crash and continued to take the corners as fast as possible, driving as if every second mattered. Never mind the time wasted in the snowbank, now he had to make up for it.

I slipped into a morose state. The jeep was loud, and I could barely hear what Pete and George were saying. I tuned them out and ruminated on the stupidity of everything. It seemed that we had ventured into the backcountry overburdened with innocence, thinking that we were going to do this and that, achieve amazing feats, grab a little glory, slide through the wilderness like a playground, become more than we were and return with the stories to prove it. Instead, we had evaporated into petty squabbles and rash acts. Now Andy was gone, somewhere in nature's maw, whether alive or dead, we had no idea. So, we had fled the vast wild domain to beg for a few alms of civilization, a little help for our friend. This simple act, the asking for help, unleashed a juggernaut of mechanized response, including the death box we were locked in, hurtling down the mountain at a breakneck pace. The situation left me profoundly depressed. At least in the mountains we made the decisions and endured the consequences. We no longer made any decisions; we handed that over to the forces of law and order.

I was jerked out of my gloom when Pete drove us off the road again, sliding on a patch of tarmac wet from snowmelt. The jeep spun around and jumped into another snowbank. Again, the blow was cushioned, so neither machine nor subjects were injured. But we were stuck. If Pete wasn't a cop, armed to the teeth, I would have been hard-pressed to curb my tongue. Instead, fatalism took over and I accepted the accident with a shrug, clambering out of the back seat to survey the new project.

We seemed to have exhausted our allotment of random good citizens. Since the last incident, we'd seen no other traffic. For now, we were on our own. Once again, we dug snow from under the tires and jammed in sticks. Pete remained enthusiastic, directing the proceedings with abundant cheer. I kept my mouth shut and did what he told me. There was something colonial about the scene: a clean-cut cop with his ragged lackeys. He favored George with his attempts at conversation, but then George had the more respectable presentation. Despite the long hair and tattered clothes, George radiated health and a positive character. I had greasy, shoulder-length hair and looked haunted. That, and my inclination toward sarcasm made me an object of suspicion for Pete. Who knew what I was up to, really? It was hard to tell what Pete thought about us because climbers are often regarded with a complicated awe: a mixture of admiration for their courage and dismissal for their presumed insanity. Whatever was going on in Pete's brain, he was our boss, and we did what he said.

With a pathway of sticks for each set of tires, we watched Pete gun the jeep back out of the snow and onto the road. The scheme worked; we had become a well-oiled team. I climbed back into the jeep with reluctance, but after the second crash Pete got the message and he drove with prudence the rest of the way.

Things were moving so fast that I felt dazed. As George and Pete talked, I withdrew. I didn't understand exactly what the sheriff's department wanted from us. Pete had made vague comments about the rescue plan when he picked us up, enough to indicate that we would play a part in the operations. But what part? After a series of radio conversations with the dispatcher at the sheriff's headquarters, he announced that we were going directly to the helipad where the rescue was moving into the King's Canyon backcountry. While the team set up a base camp at the mouth of Silver Creek, George and I would fly over the drainage and look for Andy. The opportunity to take a helicopter flight into the mountains drove a spike into my anxiety. Acrophobia had been a constant for most of my life. When I started rock climbing, the first time or two it had been so intense that I thought my skull would explode. Then something shifted and the panic burned away, at least enough to climb. But climbing had a logical relationship with exposure: working from the ground up, there was a progressive desensitization to the height, and it wasn't such a bother. Sudden exposure, though, like walking to the edge of a cliff, that still gave me a fluttering in the bowels. The idea of flying in a helicopter terrified me and taking part in the aerial survey made me want to run away. Not that there was any escape from the clutches of the sheriff's department. We had asked for a rescue and a flyover and that's exactly what we were going to get. I shuddered, struggling to accept the conditions. I kept coming back to one thing: if it led to getting Andy out of the wilderness in one piece, okay; it was worth it.

We emerged from the mountains into foothills of oak chaparral. At the lower elevations, the air was dry, and the breeze was hot. A series of backroads led us to the top of a ridge with a large open area, graded flat and covered with gravel. Half a dozen official trucks and vans were parked. I saw no activity except for a large man standing next to a pickup, smoking a cigar. We got out and were introduced to the sheriff. He wanted to hear more details of our story, some of which Pete had gotten from George and radioed down to dispatch as we drove, in between crashes.

The sheriff was in uniform, but I thought that he would look like a sheriff without it: a big, burly guy with a handlebar mustache and a drawling way of talking that led me to assume he had grown up in a John Wayne movie. He seemed keen on assessing whether we were disreputable or not.

"So, what were you all doing back there, anyway? That's God's country." This would not be the last time we would hear this pronouncement, uttered in such a way as to suggest that it was a country only for a god, which clearly, we were not.

George gave a brief summary of our interest in climbing new routes in Tehipite Valley; sensing the probing nature of the question, he threw in that we had come down from Yosemite where we had been climbing for a while. I nodded along, trying to look pensive and mature.

"So, you all have done this kind of thing before, have you?" The sheriff's flinty eyes sought to penetrate into our souls as he probed for clues to our character.

George revealed that he and Andy had recently climbed El Capitan, a feat so prestigious that even a flatlander would be impressed. I could tell by a flicker of the sheriff's eyelids that he understood the significance of this achievement, and he immediately started to treat us with respect. I hoped I would not have to cite my credentials, which were thinner and would not help our presentation. I could imagine the sheriff's reaction if I started talking about chess and how my winning ways factored into this whole chain of events. It might be evidence for the disreputable category. This train of thought prompted me to imagine headlines in the Fresno Bee: "Stalemate in King's Canyon: Lost Chess Player Emerges With Missing Pieces."

"Well, boys, we'll be bringing in a chopper here pretty quick. It's a two-seater, so we'll take you in one at a time. You can scout for your buddy on the way in. We've already got a camp started down on the Middle Fork. The chopper will drop you there so you can help the rescue team. We've got some really good men in there. Lots of experience, they know what they're doing. Your job'll be to point 'em in the right direction. All right, good luck to you." With that, the sheriff dropped the stump of his cigar, shook hands with the expected crushing grip, then jumped in his F350 highboy truck and roared off in a spray of gravel.

Pete looked at us with a mixture of sheepishness and pride, as if acknowledging that his boss was an acquired taste. "Good man," was all he said.

[g]   George and I wandered up to a high point on the ridge. Staring across the foothills to the distant mountains, we faced the direction of our lost comrade, many miles away. I knew we both thought about him, and I tried to feel his spirit, if any spirit was left, some spark that would give me hope. But the mountains gave nothing.

"George, what the hell are we doing?"

"I know, this is nuts, huh? But at least we get the flyover. If he's pinned down, even if we don't spot him right away, he'll hear the chopper, he'll make a signal. Besides, we have to go back for our stuff. Now we get a ride."

"Yeah. Well, you can go first. Being around cops makes me nervous."

"Me too, but these guys seem all right. They're having fun, playing with gear. You worried about the weed?"

"Shit!" I had forgotten about the two ounces of grass stuffed into my big pack and stored inside our tent in Little Tehipite Valley. It was well hidden and there was no reason for any of the sheriff's squad to root around in our stuff. As long as we weren't blowing smoke in their faces, they wouldn't know about it. Still, I didn't relish the thought of holding that much weed while surrounded by cops.

Pete yelled that the helicopter was coming. Within minutes we could hear the throbbing beat of its rotors as it flew over the forest. It was surprisingly small, just like the sheriff said, a two-seater. A single bubble of Plexiglas formed the pilot and passenger compartment. It was loud and dramatic, but it looked like a toy as it set down on the packed dirt of the helipad. The pilot didn't shut down the rotors and the chopper danced on its skids, barely on the ground, eager to be off again. A gesture from the pilot spurred George to grab his pack and run, ducking his head to stay under the blades. He jumped in without looking back. As soon as he was strapped in, the chopper vibrated with increasing intensity and lifted off the ground amid flying dust and a hellish cacophony. A minute later, it was gone.

Pete walked over and asked if I was hungry, waving his hand at a stack of boxes next to the white rescue van. I knew it was the rescue van because it was emblazoned with the sheriff's shield and the word RESCUE was painted in bold letters on the front, back, and the sides. It was one of those vans where the sidewalls were covered with different sized compartment doors like on fire trucks. As I walked over to the van, Pete opened one of the panels to reveal at least a dozen full coils of climbing rope. The compartment was a climber's dream. Ropes were quite expensive and if you took a single big fall, the rope had to be discarded. Acquiring gear was a challenge for climbing bums and admiring the sheriff's stash reminded me of when I shoplifted a new rope from the climbing store in Yosemite. It was one of those desperation moves, probably not good for my karma, but I had a friend who worked in the store and he agreed to let me take it out the back while he looked the other way. Not that I had designs on the sheriff's gear, but just looking at it left me feeling impoverished.

I turned away from the truck and its material wealth. I didn't need anything else to feel depressed about. Walking off without a word, I hoped that Pete was too busy fiddling with his ropes to notice my agitation. Yet I didn't care enough to try harder to be normal. I wasn't normal, anyway, and I didn't like cops. After what happened in Louisiana, why should I? I'd have to be crazy. I certainly wasn't going to confide in Pete, who didn't strike me as too bright. It was easy to imagine his scornful reaction to my angst.

I had no idea how long it would take before the chopper returned, but it occurred to me that it could be an hour or two. My nerves were on a fuse and if something didn't change, I'd explode. Or implode, more likely. It occurred to me that food might offer a reliable distraction. I wandered back over to the van and the stack of brown cartons.

Opening the lid of the top carton, I found inside tightly packed brown boxes about the size of a small loaf of bread. Stenciled on the top of these boxes were the words MEAL, COMBAT, INDIVIDUAL. Under this cheerful headline were subtitles advertising the nature of the contents. One said,

BEANS AND WIENERS, another BEEFSTEAK, POTATOES, AND GRAVY, and yet another promised, HAM AND LIMA BEANS. It was not a festive array. I peeked inside a different box and saw more neat stacks, but this time of cans, all a curious bronze color with no wrappers, just more stenciled names of common food items. Having avoided the draft, I'd dodged the world of military sustenance. In my ignorance, I assumed that the food in the cans would resemble the lackluster food in supermarket cans.

Pete saw me staring at the cans in the box. "C-rations. Not bad. Take what you want."

He opened another panel in the truck and found a small container, pulled out a P-38 can opener, and tossed it in my direction. I scrambled to catch it, bumping into the stack of ration boxes, knocking one to the ground and failing to grab the opener as it flew past. While Pete smirked, I replaced the box and picked up the P-38. Backpackers used the same tool, a thumb-sized, hand-cranked can opener developed by the Army so their soldiers had a foolproof means of getting to the grub. Simply puncture and crank the blade in and out, walking the opener around the can's perimeter. Even though it was an Army product, this humble tool remains the best can opener ever devised, if you don't mind a little workout for your fingers.

I selected a box advertising HAM AND LIMA BEANS, for a moment remembering the lima beans that my mother served and feeling a spark of nostalgia for the home front. At the first puncture of the lid, I detected a peculiar odor that did not remind me of home. I scooped out a spoonful of the congealed glop, feeling committed and even a bit curious. It didn't taste like my mother's cooking. Although I had never eaten canned dog food, I imagined that it wasn't far from HAM AND LIMA BEANS. I was hungry, so I maneuvered the gunk into my mouth and swallowed it, bite after bite until the can was empty. I didn't want to offend Pete and I figured he'd laugh at me if I spit it out, even though that was my inclination.

After I finished the can, I pulled out its neighbor, which claimed to be fruit cocktail. It was filled with sugary goo interspersed with pastel-colored lumps that could have been fruit at some point of origin. By this time, it had transformed into a gelatinous sludge devoid of taste, but possible to swallow. So, I swallowed. Rude or not, one bite was enough.

Pete opened another panel in the van where there was a garbage bag, and I deposited the cans before wandering away to sit on a rock. I wanted a joint, badly.

Soon enough I could hear the helicopter coming back. Pete gave me the high sign and I picked up my pack and walked over to the edge of the helipad.

The helicopter landed with a dusty, deafening racket. I trotted over in a crouch, dragging my pack, and climbed in, shoving my fear down as hard as I could. Once in the machine, the pilot showed me how to buckle the harness and don headphones so we could talk despite the din. It was not a reassuring machine. As we lifted off, I thought it seemed like nothing more than a flying golf cart, very tiny and hardly something to conquer the sky. The Plexiglas cockpit was alarming. I could see out on all sides and right between my feet. The sense of exposure made rock climbing feel like kiddie stuff. I recognized that I couldn't allow myself to show weakness by freaking out and demanding to be returned to the ground; I'd never live down the shame. I already carried plenty and didn't need more, so I kept my mouth shut and tried to act like a pro. Besides, it was too late: we were airborne.

As we flew east and dropped into the long valley of the Middle Fork, I forced myself to appreciate the panorama. It was a spectacle of mythic proportions. Everywhere there were rock cliffs, spires, slabs and domes, more granite than trees as far as I could see. The Middle Fork had carved a deep valley and the tributaries were all precipitous. That we had thought to walk freely in this landscape seemed presumptuous; from the air it looked as if you would need the fortitude of Hercules. I consumed the view and wanted to be cool about how mind-blowing it was, but the gorges and rocks played with the air, shaping abrupt gusts and whirls that burst out of every direction. Each wind blast shoved the helicopter to one side, then back to the other, or pushed down from above, and our progress through the turbulence felt like bouncing along whitewater rapids. The pilot flew the chopper as if it were an insect, constantly correcting its course with sudden maneuvers. I wanted to vomit. Nausea and panic threatened to overwhelm me; both had to be repressed with brute force. Before long I was exhausted, silently mouthing oaths that I would never leave the ground again.

Landmarks have a different appearance from the air, but I recognized the Silver Creek drainage when we got to it and felt a morbid twinge of regret that this rough, wild landscape now felt tainted. The pilot turned the ship, and we flew up the tributary, stopping to hover over the gorge. The gorge made sharp turns upstream and down and framed a circular space in between, like a roofless chamber. The granite here was dark, a kind of sooty rock that looked like slate. I looked down into a perilous eye of water-formed rock. The walls of the eye were hundreds of feet high, giving the impression of staring into a black hole. I shuddered and looked away. I scanned the rocky slopes and sparse timber above the gorge walls. I saw nothing. I saw no sleeping bag spread out for signal, no tent fly, no sign of human existence. There was nothing to see at all except for another array of rocks, trees and water. It was then that I knew Andy was dead.

The pilot looked at me and I shrugged my shoulders. He nodded and spun the ship around, quickly taking us down Silver Creek and into the Middle Fork valley. On the other side of the river from Silver Creek was a flat spot with a meadow. As we came in for landing, I could see that the sheriff's department had already established a base camp among the trees. I couldn't get out of the helicopter fast enough and trotted over to see George.

He was in no mood to celebrate my return to the ground. "Come on, let's go get our stuff. We're gonna need it anyway and it's getting dark." It had only been this morning that we had arisen from exhausted slumber in a remote wilderness cabin, hiked like maniacs to get out, called the cops, crashed our way down the mountains in a jeep, just to fly back to the wilderness in a preposterous whirligig, and now George wanted to mount an expedition to retrieve the gear we'd left before we started this circular odyssey.

"What about the river, George?"

"No sweat. These guys are like hyped-up Boy Scouts... they already have a rope crossing rigged up."

"What! How the hell did they do that?"

"That was my question! Apparently, they put a guy in pads and a life vest, then told him to swim the river, dragging a rope. Of course, he ended up way downstream, but he made it across. They pulled the rope tight, hung a bosun's chair, and now we have our own Tyrolean traverse." I could see that George was pumped at the prospect of trying out this rig, but his urgency also expressed something deeper. I knew I should stop resisting. We both needed to reclaim a little autonomy.

"Sure, man. Let's do it."

The rope traverse over the river was a standard rescue rig known as a "highline." Climbers call them Tyrolean traverses and have used them for decades as a temporary means to cross back and forth over empty space. Across the Middle Fork, there was one line, known as the track line, stretched as taut as possible between two trees and well above the water level. From this was suspended a bosun's chair, a perch used for working on the masts and rigging of ships. The chair was not much of a chair, basically just a small board. The board hung from a pulley that ran on the track line. You wriggled as much of your ass as would fit onto the board, then sat suspended from the pulley. Progress across the river was made by pulling on the track line, dragging the seat and you along with it. It could have been fun except that it was hard work.

George was eager to get on the rope, so I lagged behind. He slid into the bosun's chair, ignoring an attempt by one of the rescue cops to provide instructions, and began hauling himself over with his considerable arm strength. That left me to mill around with the cops while they talked about George with skepticism. Their pedantic judgments reminded me of why I didn't like cops or rescue workers. They were mired in black and white, like chess pieces, unable to see beyond the board.

Rescue people are obsessed with safety, admirable in some respects but a path to dogmatic thinking. This tendency toward rigidity permeates everything they do, leaving them with a neurotic fatalism. Do as I say, or you will die; the terms are always certain. I had encountered this type before. When Carrot and I had climbed the main glacier route on Mt. Baker in the North Cascades, as a party of two we had to pass a cluster of twenty or thirty mountaineers on the lower slopes. We stopped to say hi, wondering what they were doing, since the summit was still a long way. They were standing around practicing rescue maneuvers while trying to decide whether to push on or retreat because of the light cloud cover. They marveled that there were only two of us. Clouds were building up, they said. I surveyed the sky and thought there was as much chance things would clear as get worse. We said we were pushing on. Although their leader said nothing, I could see the "tsk, tsk" word balloons floating above his shoulders as he shook his head in admonishment. Carrot and I resumed trekking up the ice, but before we were out of earshot, the leader called out, "Don't let your ambition overcome your precaution!" I waved and we turned on the speed in order not to run into them again. The rest of the climb passed without incident and the weather was lovely from the summit, which we had to ourselves.

George made it to the other side of the river, so I abandoned my reverie and focused on not making a fool of myself on the highline. I used the retrieval line to pull the chair back and took my turn hauling ass over the drink. Despite the critical audience,

I made it across in reasonable style. I had to give them credit, they'd rigged it well.

George and I retraced our steps along the east shore, the same route we had walked two days ago after going to the mouth of Silver Creek looking for a sign of Andy and finding nothing. The walk back to our campsite had been heavy with anxious despair. Now, I still carried the despair, but I felt less anxious. Before, we'd been filled with uncertainties—no longer. I said as much to George.

"Did you see anything on your flight? I didn't. He can't be alive."

"Shit, I know what you mean. I didn't see anything either. And we spent a while looking into that drainage, got as low as we could, but there was nothing. I don't even see where the hell he would have gone. Big walls down in there, waterfalls, no line of weakness. Impossible. We couldn't even get down very low, there just wasn't room to maneuver the chopper safely. Not a nice place."

"So, where the fuck is he?"

"Dunno. Fell into a crevice somewhere, or under a boulder, something that makes it hard to see from the air."

"What a fucking asshole. Son of a bitch. Damn him!"

"I know, I know. Shoulda stayed with us, the stubborn shithead. I've seen him get like that before. We got into a jam on the Salathe and it was looking like we weren't gonna make our bivvy ledge. Andy got super intense, took the lead, and just powered up the next pitch, mostly in the dark. It was either that or spend the night hanging in slings. I tried to talk him out of that then, too, but... I guess it worked out."

"Ahh, George, I miss the bastard."

"Yeah. Me, too."

I spied our tent through the trees, and as we approached, I experienced a surge of hope that maybe Andy would be sitting there, smiling at stupid old us. But he wasn't.

We packed up the tent and our gear, including the pot stash, jamming it all hastily into the big packs. Dusk had arrived and we wanted to negotiate the rope bridge before dark, so we shouldered the loads and hiked back. While I waited for George to cross, I stared into the dark, curving walls of the Silver Creek gorge. Peering into the gloom, I felt my thoughts sucked into a grim inner reservoir. The gravity of despair had me in its grip.

[h]   I expected to wake up the next morning to bugle calls, but all I heard was a plaintive dove and the churning river. I lay motionless in the sleeping bag, trying to gather my wits. George breathed with the slow rhythm of sleep. Eventually, I picked out the noise of dishes rattling on the other side of the camp, noise that led me to expect it wouldn't be long before the aroma of coffee filtered through the pines. Last night, after crossing the river, George and I had carried our stuff through the middle of camp and to the far side, finding a place within the trees distant enough from the cops so they wouldn't be in our faces. I was glad for the distance; it gave me a chance to ignore the stirring of the rescue squad, burrow deeper into my bag, and hope that the day would become something besides what I knew it was going to be.

George snorted and twitched, signs of a waking animal. I gave him a nudge. "George. Time for reveille. Rise and shine, soldier!"

George groaned and turned away, but soon sat up. "Shit," was all he said.

The inside of the tent was a mess. Piles of climbing gear were mixed with clothes, food bags, cook stove, water bottles, fuel canisters, toilet paper, and a copy of Aldous Huxley's *Point Counter Point* ripped down the spine so we could both read it. There was barely enough room for the sleeping bags and the décor resembled a packrat nest. We were supposed to have two tents, but then Andy had the other one. Wherever it was.

We extricated ourselves from the tent, one at a time. I went first with a roll of toilet paper and hiked up into the woods to dig a cat hole under a tree. I hoped that by the time I got back George would already be talking to the cops and I could just slide in without having to think of something to say.

Brad was the leader of the field operations. He was a deputy sheriff, a big man with a solid physique. Like the sheriff, he also had a handlebar moustache, perhaps a requirement in these parts for serious law enforcement types. I gathered that the rescue team consisted of police officers who had been pulled from other assignments. Young and fit, for them it was a junket. Aside from offering significant amounts of overtime, the opportunity to cavort around in the wilds with unlimited gear and tactical support made this a welcome duty. I couldn't blame them. In Yosemite there was a national park rescue team made up of rangers, but when rescues got technical, they usually recruited experienced climbers from Camp 4. The climbers in 4 were, after all, experts on getting around in Yosemite's vertical environment. Any climber recruited for these events was happy to go, not only because it was the right thing to do, to render assistance to a fellow mountaineer, but because there was good money in it.

Brad barked out directions to the assembled crew, about twelve of us, as we stood around the campfire in a circle. He had a large walkie-talkie in his hand that he waved around for emphasis. Most of the cops held mugs of steaming coffee like shields in front of their faces. George and I didn't drink coffee, so we passed a water bottle back and forth. Brad wanted half the crew to push into Silver Creek. The goal would be to look for Andy's body, or, as he called it, "the subject remains."

"If we locate the subject, or any items belonging to the subject, immediately radio back here to the advanced operations base. Then, and only then, we'll determine how to proceed. Do not disturb any remains until we can catalog the location and condition. Do not go off on your own. Do not, I repeat, do not do anything stupid. If you don't know if it's stupid, then don't do it. It's rugged country out there. God's country. Last I looked, nobody here is God. Don't even try. Be a team. Be safe." Brad rattled off each word like heavy machine gun fire, articulated at a precise cadence to prevent jamming. "All right, men, we've got a job to do. Grab some grub. We're heading out at 0800." Brad and all the cops looked at their watches. George and I didn't have watches, so we looked at each other and shrugged.

Brad would stay at what he called "the advanced operations base" where he would use the big radio to maintain contact with the search crew as well as central dispatch at the sheriff's office down in Fresno. Another deputy, a guy named Jarvis, would be in charge of the Silver Creek reconnaissance. I didn't know if Jarvis was his first name or last name, no one called him anything else. He was a wiry fellow, short and muscular, decked out in fatigues and a ball cap that said "BITE ME." He looked like someone I didn't want to mess with, but he turned out to have a wit to him. As he named off the six cops to fill out his team, which included me and George, he gave us a slight, ironic smile. "Glad you boys are here. We're a little thin on the technical side of things," and he winked. We chuckled, then wondered what he meant.

It looked like we'd be heading out soon, but we had enough time to eat some grub. There was a stack of Army rations near the squad's propane stove, and we detoured there before heading to our tent, each grabbing a box labeled "BREAKFAST UNIT." Back in our space, I sat cross-legged and pulled out a can of scrambled eggs. Once opened, I took an exploratory bite. Certainly, I could have eaten more, but I chose not to. It made me think of what it might be like to chew old flip-flops.

George watched me until he could no longer hold down the giggles. He tossed his can up and down in one hand like a juggling ball. "What is this fucking shit?"

"That would be the question, now, wouldn't it?"

He let the can fall to the ground and glared at it. "Jesus Christ."

"Yeah, it's at least that ancient. I recommend proceeding directly to the biscuits." The canned biscuits, which were similar to Ritz crackers, were closer to my expectations of food. I crunched down a handful while throwing a water bottle and an extra shirt in my day pack.

"I'm bringing some gorp; fuck that crap." George loved his gorp. Primarily a mixture of granola, dried fruit, and chocolate chips, he carried it around like a feed bag, stopping for regular infusions. Many would consider it a monotonous diet, but I envied him. Mired in even simpler habits, I'd only brought a sack of shelled sunflower seeds, a sack of raisins, and a tube of honey. I knew George would share his gorp because that's the way he was. And I, in turn, would share the honey and seeds. We didn't need the Army's notion of food.

When we got to the rope bridge Jarvis was already sending his men across, closely supervised by Brad, who offered a barrage of last-minute instructions. Jarvis ignored Brad, as if he wasn't there. After his crew had crossed, Jarvis waved us on to the highline. He came over last and promptly took the lead, marching his troop single file down the shore in the direction of Silver Creek. George and I fell in at the end of the line.

We walked into a tangle of brush and rocks when we came to the mouth of Silver Creek. Pushing through, we worked our way upstream. In ten minutes, we arrived at the gorge, where the walls closed in, the creek narrowed, and the way forward was uncertain. We stopped to gauge the prospects. The walls rose straight out of the creek, fifty feet high, framing the entrance to the gorge like a portal. A torrent of pools and rapids swirled past these walls, wrapping around giant boulders that shaped the flow. The only way forward involved wading the shallows along the edge of the wall, hoping that it didn't drop off into a pool. We filed into the ankle-deep water, stepping carefully.

We didn't get far. Jarvis stopped where the vertical wall met the full depth of the creek. The morning sun never reached into this niche, and it was a chilly, foreboding place. The pool was too deep to wade and too cold to swim. We stood together and wondered what to do while Jarvis radioed back to base. We had barely started our foray, had gotten nowhere, and learned nothing. Except that Silver Creek was not going to give away its secrets.

Jarvis signaled to George and me. "Brad thinks we ought to scout both sides of the creek to see if there is any way over these walls and into the back of the gorge. I'm wondering if we should split up."

I felt lead in my bones and a lassitude of spirit, but George piped up, "We know this side a bit because we came down it already. The two of us can go back up the slope and scout for a way into the upper gorge."

Jarvis studied George's face. Clearly, he admired his confidence. "All right. I'll take the rest of the boys and cross over the creek. We'll check out the other side, see if there's any way through all this fuckin' rock. I don't have a radio for you, so you'll have to be careful. Don't take risks. If you find any lines of weakness, keep in mind it has to be practical for a rescue team to use. No rock climbing. We'll rendezvous back at base."

"Sounds good."

"Be safe."

I couldn't believe our good fortune in getting away from the cops again. I could have hugged George for his ingenuity. While Jarvis and his boys contemplated what they would need to do to get to the other side of the creek, George and I took off without hesitation. We scrambled back down to the river, turned upstream, then as soon as the slope became less rocky, we angled uphill, aiming toward that same gap we came over on the way down four days before. It seemed like last year. We stayed as close to the Silver Creek drainage as we could, but the steep granite formed an extensive buttress system and we were repeatedly forced back toward our original descent route. There wasn't going to be a shortcut into the gorge.

It was getting close to midday by the time we made it back to the saddle at the top of the ridge. We sat down for a drink of water and some snacks. I pulled out my seeds and raisins, offering them to George. He shook his head, munched on his gorp for a while, then wordlessly passed me his bag. I nodded in gratitude and took a handful.

"What now?" I asked with a full mouth.

"Dunno. Doesn't look like a good way into the gorge to me. You know we could have done a simple traverse along the wall over that pool. Big jugs for handholds, would've been easy."

"Yeah, I don't think they're too comfortable with climbing."

"To say the least. Since we're up here I suppose we could explore down toward the top of the gorge walls, see if there is any way through, or maybe some sign of Andy."

"Yeah. Might as well. I'm in no hurry to get back to the *advanced operations base*."

George snorted, "Yeah, what the fuck, huh?"

We hiked down from the saddle toward the upper reaches of the gorge, going down into the terrain that swallowed Andy. It was steep, rocky, and slow going. Not only were there vast slabs of granite but also eroded expanses of loose rock and broken bits of exfoliated plates crumbling into gravel. We explored tentatively, finding more loose rock the lower we got, conscious that a slip could turn into a slide impossible to arrest before one hurtled over the lip of the wall below. We imagined what it would be like to negotiate this terrain with a heavy pack.

"Holy shit!" I yelled as I jerked to a halt and put my arms out to stop George from stepping around me. Four feet ahead lay a large, coiled rattlesnake, taut and ready to strike, buzzing its warning.

"Damn!" George peered over my shoulder and yielded as I backed into him. I was already out of range of a potential strike, but the intensity of a coiled viper demands as much space as you can give it. We both backed away smoothly, tendering every respect to the beast.

"That's enough to loosen your bowels," I observed.

"Yeah. Jesus. You know, with a big pack, something like that could make you lose your balance."

"Yeah." I knew what he was thinking. We were about a hundred feet above the edge of the gorge. There was nothing to stop a falling body.

We detoured around the snake and continued our probe into the drainage. It was well into the afternoon when we reached an outcrop that gave us an unrestricted view along the top of the gorge in both directions. We stopped for more water, seeds, and gorp. I pulled out a joint I had brought from the main stash back in the tent and we smoked it while we surveyed the complicated topography of Silver Creek.

"Really doesn't look good, does it?" Obvious, but I didn't know what else to say.

"It doesn't. There's no sign of him. From where we split up, he would have come down right over there. No idea where he would have gone after that."

"Yeah. Except over the edge."

"Yeah."

We hiked back to base in waning light and silence. When we got off the rope bridge and walked over to tell Jarvis that we had found nothing on our reconnaissance, I felt the eyes of the cops follow me. Since I usually tried to be invisible, this made me nervous. Jarvis received our report, but I noticed an inner tension. I obsessed, figuring that something was wrong. As soon as George finished, Jarvis motioned me to step aside. "We need to talk." Not good, I thought, not good.

"We found your dope. When you guys didn't come back sooner, some of us figured you might have bugged out, so we searched your tent."

"Bugged out?" The thought was so preposterous I didn't even know how to protest.

"Yes, sir. We don't really know you fellows, so Brad thought maybe you just took off. He thought there might be some clues to your state of mind in your stuff. Then he found the dope."

"Took off?" It seemed I could only repeat key phrases.

"Yes, sir, sorry about that. So, anyway, we agreed that if you get rid of the dope, we won't do anything about it." I could tell Jarvis wasn't entirely comfortable with the search of our tent. It was hard to understand, and the justification didn't add up. Who thinks like that? Weird hippies claiming to be climbers run away from rescuing their friend, fleeing into the mountains never to be seen again. Makes perfect sense to a certain point of view, apparently. How they filtered this through their logic centers was beyond me. We had a plan with Jarvis to scout a section of ground and that's what we did. How that got translated into the two of us disappearing into the wilderness, leaving all our precious gear, was incomprehensible.

When I told George he was stunned. "What the hell is going on?"

"Paranoid cops, man, paranoid cops. Just the way they think. Now they got me all paranoid."

"What are we gonna do?"

"Jarvis wants me to dump the dope in the campfire, burn it up. Not much choice. Fuckin' assholes. I guess I can stand in the cloud and suck it in while it burns, get a buzz that way."

"Don't do that, man, that'll just piss 'em off."

"Fuck 'em. Fuck 'em, fuck 'em, fuck 'em."

I marched over to our tent, grabbed the two baggies of weed and carried them over to the campfire. As the cops backed away, I took each bag and emptied it over the flames. With exaggerated ceremony, I leaned over the spiraling clouds of smoke and took huge breaths. The cops watched me without comment, but they watched every move. Three big inhalations and the pot was consumed. I felt the onset of a major buzz, so I grabbed two boxes of C-rations and staggered back to our tent. I dropped one box in front of George and plopped down to munch out on the other, whatever was in the box, at this point it didn't matter.

George looked at me with a bit of wonder. "You're a fuckin' maniac, you know that?"

I nodded and got to work opening cans.

[i] The next morning, we all pretended nothing had happened. Given the fruitless effort of the previous day, it wasn't clear how the rescue should proceed. After splitting up, Jarvis'

team had been unsuccessful in finding a way into the gorge on the other side of Silver Creek. It seemed impenetrable. But if Andy was anywhere, he had to be in that gorge. There weren't any other options.

Brad and the Fresno County Sheriff's team were stymied. The terrain was too much for their know-how, but they couldn't give up, not at this stage. A man was missing. Brad spent the morning on the radio to central dispatch, digging for answers. George didn't bother to share his opinion about traversing along the canyon wall above the pool. They didn't ask for opinions, anyway. I guess they didn't see much point in seeking advice from dopers who might run away into the wilderness for no reason. Beyond that pool was a rock corner; impossible to know what came after that. Could be more of the same, could be a passage. There was only one way to find out. But the sheriff's rescue team expressed discomfort with climbing, even close to the ground. They weren't going to climb rocks, that was clear. We milled around the campsite, picking at rations, drinking coffee, drinking water, chatting in distracted confusion. I followed George as he circulated through the group, nodding at his words and avoiding any conversations on my own.

Finally, Brad announced that they were bringing in a Navy aerial reconnaissance team to attempt a closer inspection of the gorge from the air. A "heli-tack re-con team," he called it. This would be a crack unit in one of their UH-1 "Huey" choppers, eager to test their mettle in devious and unforgiving terrain. The Vietnam war was going at full tilt, a war of helicopters, and I imagined that the Navy jumped at the chance to give their boys some live-action training before shipping them halfway around the world to fight in a jungle war that never seemed to end.

We were told to sit tight in camp while the re-con team did their thing. The goal was to descend straight down into the gorge as low as they could go. No one expected a landing, but maybe they would spot him from the air.

It wasn't our show. It was our friend, but we had handed off his fate to the authorities and they were in command, determined to succor a wayward soul or haul out the body. To me, the rescue was a fantasy. I believed it was only a body at this point, and I had no stomach for dragging it out of the wilderness. Let it lie, let it lie, it was past our agency. If it were me laying there, I'd rather remain in the backcountry. What was the other choice? A manicured bourgeois graveyard? The hell with the second-guessers, let nature reclaim its own.

I went back to the tent. Despite my surly mood, it was another fine day in the Sierras, so I dragged out my pad, propped it up against a tree and sat down to read more from *Point Counter Point*. I hoped for an infusion of Huxley's cynical detachment but what I read brought me right back to the bone.

> *There are confessable agonies, sufferings of which one can positively be proud. Of bereavement, of parting, of the sense of sin and the fear of death the poets have eloquently spoken. They command the world's sympathy. But there are also discreditable anguishes, no less excruciating than the others, but of which the sufferer dare not, cannot speak.*

I cringed, feeling an overflow from my own reservoir of discreditable anguish. I didn't understand what was behind this emotion, whether a forgotten deed or just a piercing suspicion of inadequacy. It burned like a radioactive core. I was unable to speak about this fire, in fact I couldn't even think of it, not then. Like most experiences of shame, closer inspection promised a doorway that, if crossed, offered no exit. Perhaps I hadn't done anything that deserved this level of affliction; all I knew was that I felt like a fraud, a pretender, and that rather than investigate the internal dissonance I preferred to push it down and bury it deeper. There was always the hope that it would never reach the surface again.

Ignoring the emotional jab of the text, I read on as the sun crept into the shade, letting the plot carry me away from challenging reflections. When the sounds of the Huey could be heard coming up the valley, I tried to ignore them. It was a good book, but even if it hadn't been, it was a shield against the society in which we were immersed. George wandered over from the camp, retrieved his pad and his half of the book from the tent, and propped himself against the nearest tree.

"Not much to see," he reported. "Chopper is up in the gorge, out of sight. Noisy thing, though, huh?"

"I hope they spot him. I want to get out of here. No way Andy's alive."

"Hard to admit, but you're probably right."

"So what's the fucking point?"

"I dunno, man, I guess they have to find the body. Can't leave a corpse to clutter up the mountains."

"Right. Like it's fucking clutter if they can't even find it. You know, I've had it with this rescue shit. I can't take much more of this. Maybe bugging out isn't such a bad idea. They'd never find us. Probably get lost trying."

"I know. Guess it's an option." George started to read but soon fell asleep in the sun.

I heard the steady whop whop of the chopper blades as the craft hovered over Silver Creek. The sound provided a counterpoint to the normal background noise of the valley: the wind in the pines, the occasional raven croak, and the steady churn of the river. The chopper sounds fluctuated with the wind and position. When they lowered the metallic beast into the gorge the walls muffled the racket, as if it were in a giant can. With half an ear I followed these sonic reports but none of them told me what was happening. I wrestled my attention into the book only to have it hauled out again with each change in the noise. Things were getting done, but what? George had the right idea, just go to sleep. Not for me, though; I had too much anxiety and no more pot.

Wherever Andy's body lay in that gorge, it was a remote niche, never visited except by a few wild creatures, a sanctuary beyond the reach of humankind. A dark and hard place, yes, but it was also beautiful, a manifestation of the natural forces that carve rock and shape it in dramatic forms. What better place to bury a climber?

Meanwhile cops and the machinery of war occupied the sanctuary. I understood why they were there; we'd summoned them ourselves. Something about it galled me and I couldn't sort it out. I kept coming back to the risks of the rescue itself, which seemed enormous. The gorge was narrow, too narrow for a helicopter. The previous year a chopper had crashed on El Capitan as it tried to retrieve stranded climbers, getting a little too close to the wall, catching the tip of the blades and plummeting thousands of feet to explode at the base. Risk is always a part of rescue work, but I rebelled at what we were doing here. For a body, assuming it could even be found. It made me mad. And below that anger, feeding it like a core meltdown, was the humiliation activated by the cops' perception of me, the doper loser, the freak who would run blindly away into the wilderness rather than face the remains of his friend. I was furious and depressed at the same time and the tension pushed me to a brink. Of what, I didn't know.

An hour or more went by and I noticed that the helicopter had left. I scanned the cops' end of camp but saw no bustle of activity, just guys sitting around drinking coffee. I figured that meant there was no breakthrough.

Soon Jarvis came striding over to our tent. He seemed to be the official mediator, the interpreter between the respectable cops and the hippie climbers. I wondered if he inherited this role by default. The rest of them stayed away from our tent, perhaps afraid of what they might find.

"Hey, Jarvis. Navy flew the coop?"

"Yes, sir. Negative recon, I'm afraid."

"God. What's next?" George stirred to wakefulness and propped his head up with an elbow so he could listen.

"The Navy ship is making a run in with more supplies..." Jarvis paused for the punchline, "and a crew of technical rescue experts."

"What?!" George and I spit out the same response.

"Yes, sir. Some hotshots, what I hear."

"Military?"

"I only know what they tell me. You can ask them yourselves; they'll be here shortly." With that report, he turned and sauntered back to the other side of the camp.

"A new development." I couldn't keep the sarcasm at bay. It wasn't hard to imagine the expert crew: Coast Guard elite in full tactical gear, ready to show the kids how it's done.

George, however, was excited again. "I wonder who they're bringing in? Hope it's somebody with the chops to get into the gorge."

"That would be relevant."

George grinned and bounced to his feet. "I hear the chopper. Let's go check out the new heroes."

"If you say so."

The Huey landed in the clearing beyond the trees, about a hundred yards from camp. George and I waited by the fire, hoping to see the crew of rescue experts without being seen ourselves, giving us a chance to size them up. We heard the chopper lift off and as it cleared the trees, Brad emerged from the woods leading four guys with packs. From a distance we could tell that every one of them had long hair. As they strolled into camp, I felt a shock of grateful recognition; we knew them. They were our climbing buddies from Yosemite.

[j] "What the fuck are you doing here?" George and I sounded like a chorus. Laughter followed, and backslapping, but mostly we stood in a circle and grinned at each other. Brad drifted off, shaking his head. We didn't care what the cops thought; we were

exhilarated to see familiar faces: Drone, Tubbs, Crazy Ron, and my old friend Kid Carrot.

Tubbs, the charismatic facilitator, laughed again, a healing laugh, the best laugh I'd ever heard, "How the hell are you boys?"

Before we could reply, Drone said, "Fuckin' A, you assholes. We're here to save the day."

Not to be outdone in the banter, Carrot quipped, "What's with all the cops?"

"Wait, wait. What are you guys *doing* here?" It was like a miracle; we couldn't understand it.

Drone answered, "We got the word that you guys were in the shit. Andy was lost, and a rescue started. So, we climbed into the jeep and drove down to the sheriff's department in Fresno, told them we were the official Yosemite Search and Rescue team. We said: We know this guy and we want in. Like now."

"Oh, we just fucking demanded to be flown in, we didn't even discuss it," Tubbs said.

I could hardly contain my glee. "And they flew you in, just like that? The Yosemite Search and Rescue Team?"

"Just like that, *amigo*." Tubbs' use of the Spanish reminded me of our first meeting in the hills of New Mexico a few years back. Carrot and I had made the trek south from Seattle, looking for adventure. Drone was there, too, and soon we were all climbing the local crags because they'd discovered it was as good a high as heroin. A year later, Drone and I spent a whole season in Yosemite and got to be good friends trying to climb things too hard for us. I'd met Ron in Seattle but didn't really know him. I'd heard that he was ex-Special Forces just back from Vietnam.

Everybody agreed that he was a great guy: intense, legendary, and a little unhinged. Perfect material for a climber.

These scalawags had presented themselves at the Sheriff's headquarters as the Yosemite Search and Rescue team. Hard to imagine how they sold that. Yet here they were in all their shaggy weirdness. George and I led them over to our tent and invited them to stake out their own shelters. This act finalized the essential camp dichotomy: cops on one side, hippies on the other.

Crazy Ron was the first to scout out the new boxes of rations that came in with the Huey. Having recent military experience, he knew what to expect. After a foray, he sauntered into our part of the camp, his arms full of cans he had removed from their unit boxes. He dumped them on the ground and held one up: the stenciled letters said POUND CAKE.

"Stuff's all shit, all of it. Except for the pound cake. It's actually not too bad."

Tubbs asked, "Did you just cream those boxes for the pound cake? And left the rest?"

"Somethin' like that. There's more. You might want to do the same before anyone else gets to them."

The rest of us ran over to the stacks of new rations and ransacked the remaining boxes, removing the pound cake. We took it all. The new guys grabbed some full boxes as well because they were skeptical about subsisting on pound cake. We listened closely as Ron offered tips on the proper triage of C-ration edibility. How far you went down the list depended on how desperate you were for something besides cake.

We sat in a loose circle back at the tents and stuffed down the chow. I ate cake and sunflower seeds. One way or another we filled our bellies. Looking up from his empty cans, Drone was pensive and stroked his moustache with a sly touch. He looked at me with the hint of a smile, a look that surfaced when he wanted someone to do something for him. "So... how about a doobie? Feels like that time of day, doesn't it? I know you're holding. We left our stash in the jeep. Weren't quite sure what the scene would be like, you know? But the cops are way over there, I don't think they'll pay any notice to a little smoke, do you?"

"Mmmm, there *is* a problem."

"A problem? You smoked it already?" Drone didn't want to consider a problem.

I told the story of how the cops had thought we bugged out, so they searched the tent, found the weed, made me burn it, and I inhaled two ounces in a minute. There was silence at first.

"Jesus fucking shit."

"You are kidding, right?"

"You mean we have to do this straight?"

And so on around the circle. Tubbs, however, was thoughtful. "This will need to be set right, gentlemen. Before we are done here."

"What do you mean?"

"Oh, we'll just keep our eyes open for now. But it will be set right."

We glared across the campsite, watching the cops go about their evening routine. It was like staring down the board at the white pieces, all arrayed against us, and so far, having their way. Black, however, newly reinforced, was still in the game. The unexpected arrival of our comrades lifted my spirits, but I still felt tied to an anchor sinking into the darkness. My hearty banter was one thin line away from hysteria. I had to keep a tight lid; it would be terminally uncool to lose it now. Bad enough to be exposed to the cops, but not to my friends. No way.

As usual, Carrot had the last say. "Well, fuck that, then. What have you got to read?" I pointed to George, who tore off the first few chapters of *Point Counter Point* and handed them to Carrot. He solemnly accepted the tattered pages and turned to read as much as he could by the fading light.

[k]   The next morning, I woke with an awkward mixture of hope and dread. At least our friends were with us. They brought an immediate sense of community; I don't care how odd. Carrot's presence was especially welcome. I'd known him since junior high school, and we understood each other. We'd been on the high school chess team, playing without distinction but with passion, proud of our sport. We had hung together in adolescent oblivion, sharing endless opinionated conversations about science fiction, music, politics, culture, female anatomy, or whatever crossed our minds. It was reassuring to have someone around who knew me, because I didn't feel like I knew myself at all. Waves of despair lapped at the edge of my thoughts, and I wanted nothing other than to curl into a ball and float away— either that or scream and smash things, whatever might resolve the tension.

In the face of internal dilemma, I usually tended toward paralysis. Growing up, my mother said what a good boy I was; she said it so often I think I believed it. Yet I wanted to be a rebel, tough and cool and beyond the pressures of conforming to norms that I despised, beyond caring what anyone thought. I wanted to be bad, but not exactly; I wanted to be good but look bad. It wasn't an ebb and flow, these currents of good and bad, instead they formed a vortex, an eddy frozen in space, a cycling tension that left me incapable of coherent thought or action. The longer it lasted, the crazier I felt, until I collapsed under the gravity of self-loathing. When the shit got bad, I ran and hid, as far away as I could get. However long it took, I just waited it out.

I pushed down the rumination rattling my head and crawled out of the tent. Tubbs and Ron were already up, stacking their cans of pound cake, building pyramids and other structures, every now and then opening a can and eating it.

Tubbs smiled between bites of cake. "You look like hell, amigo."

"Yeah, thanks. I'm done with this shit, man. Andy's dead and we should just let him stay where he is, wherever that is. I'm not into the circus."

"That bad?"

"That bad. Fucking cops don't know what they're doing. They won't climb rock at all, and there's no way into that gorge without scrambling or traversing or something. I just don't see the point anymore. Andy's gone. Why take the risks?"

Ron looked at me sharply, but spoke with gentleness, "I dunno, man. In Nam we always tried to get our guys out, dead or alive."

"Yeah, but this ain't Nam. He's dead, how does it matter where his body rots?"

"I hear that. But in Nam we shipped the bodies home where they belong, not left to lay in some rat shit jungle on the other side of the planet. And we certainly didn't want the VC to have the satisfaction of carving up our boys for trophies." As he talked, I could see Ron's thoughts start to slip away into the past.

"I guess."

Ron shook off the trance and continued his argument, "His family will want to decide where he rests. I think that's why the cops want to get the body out. Families expect it."

"Yeah. Still, how many risks do we take for a body? When do we say enough? What the hell is wrong with just decaying back into the earth? Why the fuss about burials and funerals and coffins and all that bullshit?" I could hear myself getting shrill.

"Chain of command, eh? Not our call. Relax, we're here, we're gonna find him and we're gonna get him out, alive or not," Ron's statement was so confident that it seemed already true.

Tubbs agreed. "Absofuckinglutely."

I laughed, but inside I shook my head, staggering under a burden of doubt. I couldn't stop thinking about the last time I saw Andy and the senseless argument we had. Why couldn't we convince him to stay with us? Did we even try? As often as I replayed the events, I couldn't figure out why things had gone the way they did. Like a moth to the flame, I was compelled to the torment. Running away would be contemptible, but that was exactly what I wanted to do. It seemed like the only way to reclaim control over my life. I shoved a piece of cake in my mouth; I didn't even taste it. For all that, it could have been ashes.

As we consumed rations, the rest of the Yosemite freaks emerged from their tents. It wasn't long before the cops took notice that we were upright. Jarvis strolled over and asked us if we were ready to try a new push into the canyon. George told him about his idea of traversing along the wall over the pool. I could see that Jarvis was impressed, though he maintained a stoic demeanor. He thought for a minute.

"Interesting idea. Out of our league, though. Here's what we can do. If you guys want to try that, we'll give you a radio and you can take a whack at it. Keep us posted along the way and let's see how far you get. I expect a safety-first priority, though. We don't need another casualty. Can you handle that?"

George smiled. "Of course."

Before long the Yosemite contingent slid across the rope bridge to the other side of the river, one after another, a hairy brigade of rescuers. We each carried a day pack with rations and water. George had the radio and took the lead. I assumed my customary place at the tail.

Across the river, we cut into the trees and aimed toward the rock buttress that framed the gorge. I could feel how the others were determined and energized. A group of tough climbers, young and strong, ready for anything, motivated by the desire to find a friend lost in the wild. We all knew and loved Andy. He was a great companion, a precious commodity, not someone to be squandered away without effort. I wanted to think like that, but it was beyond me. I didn't have the same hunger. I'd given up. Reluctant, I poked along at the end of the line, bent under the load of my dark mood.

When we came to the pool, George climbed onto the wall and started traversing along the rock, finding small hand and footholds, sometimes just above the water level. Eventually he had to ascend, following the line of least resistance, until he was over a body length above the waterline. It took him longer than I expected to traverse about a hundred feet around the pool, then he found a place where he could descend and scramble across dry boulders along the creek. He disappeared around the corner. By the time he was gone, Drone was more than halfway through the traverse, soon followed by Tubbs, Ron, and Carrot. They moved with confidence and without hesitation, but it looked sketchy to me. Parts of the traverse were wet and promised to be slippery. A fall would crash you into the jagged rocks just under the surface of the pool. I felt the anxiety mount as I watched each of my friends attempt the passage. Then it was my turn.

By the time I started, Carrot was almost at the other end of the traverse. The rest of the group had vanished around the corner. As I touched the rock, I felt my head go numb. I couldn't move. I thought about the sound I heard one day in Yosemite when a climber's body slammed into the ground headfirst. The noise was unforgettable, a squishy crunch that left nothing to the imagination.

I'd taken a few falls myself, like all climbers. The worst was unroped, the time when I plummeted sixty feet down a rock face. I banged into the wall and tumbled head over heels three times, out of control, shredding skin and breaking fingers but somehow never hitting my head or suffering injury that kept me from walking away. I've been lucky like that, even in the eighty-mile-an-hour car wreck I survived. But the sounds and sensations of bones under impact, flesh in mangling, these memories lurked in my mind like pyroclasts in a volcano, spewing forth in explosions of terror.

I imagined what it would be like to fall off the traverse, crashing into the water and rocks. I couldn't stop thinking about it. It wasn't far, but that meant nothing. Bones would break, I'd slam my skull and lose consciousness under water, every anxiety expanded to occupy all the space in my head. I struggled to reason it away. Stepping onto the foothold, my limbs shook, and I stepped back off. I stepped on, then stepped off again. I couldn't do it. I just couldn't do it. The fear was overwhelming. Time to run away, like I always did. Back down, be small, avoid the spotlight of fate. Disappear.

Carrot stopped at the end of the traverse and looked back at me, a quizzical expression on his face. I wondered what he thought about my hesitation. I waved him to go on and signaled that I was returning to camp. At this distance he wouldn't hear any words I might use to explain myself. Just as well, because I didn't have those words. I had nothing. He indicated that he got the message and turned to follow the others. I sat down on a rock, relieved, but knowing that I would pay with a coward's shame. In the end, it seemed that I was no better than the cops I scorned.

I couldn't sit there forever, so I wandered back to the rope bridge, plodding, in no hurry to get to the other side. I didn't know how I would explain any of this—it sounded crazy and weak. Excuses would be lame. As I trudged to the river, shame ripped me apart. If anyone had approached me with sympathy, I would have dissolved in tears. But that wasn't going to happen here, not the sympathy and certainly not the tears. There was no place for tears. I arranged my face into an approximation of stoic determination and walked up to the crossing. With resignation I hauled myself over the impassive might of the river. Ever vigilant, the cops spotted the activity and Brad trotted over as I unhooked from the highline rigging.

"What's the matter? Everything okay?" There was concern in his voice, but a challenge, too. Here was another irregular event featuring the strange hippie.

"Uhhh... don't... feel well," was all I could manage, muttered in a strangled voice. I avoided looking in his face, kept my head down, and slunk off to the tent. There were no further questions, and no one stopped me, but I felt the eyes on my back.

Wrung out and tired of feeling things, I shrugged off the pack, threw myself on the ground and stared through the layers of pine needles into the hard blue sky. My head filled with jagged thoughts. Each thought led to its antithesis, then cycled around to the point of origin, a squirrel cage looping over and over. Like perpetual check in a game of chess, the moves could repeat to infinity. Rules made it a draw, ending the game, but the rules didn't apply to my head. As for the clear sky, I saw an unlimited backdrop for rumination, and not much else.

Rather than facing the adversities of life head on, I usually retreated into abstractions. In time, most things went away. Books, of course, were the best shield. I'd finished the Huxley novel, but I always had something else. Couldn't run the risk of being without a book, even if it meant extra weight in the pack. From the tent, I grabbed the next volume, an already battered paperback; as soon as I touched it, I felt relief at its promise of sanctuary.

Book in hand, the weight of my failure began to fade. I opened to the first page and read.

Once you have given up the ghost, everything follows with dead certainty, even in the midst of chaos. From the beginning it was never anything but chaos: it was a fluid which enveloped me, which

I breathed in through the gills. In the substrata, where the moon shone steady and opaque, it was smooth and fecundating; above it was a jangle and a discord. In everything I quickly saw the opposite, the contradiction, and between the real and the unreal the irony, the paradox. I was my own worst enemy.

Was there no escape from self-reflection? I'd never read Henry Miller and I expected something else, something full of sex and distraction. I certainly didn't want to look any deeper into my soul. If I hadn't been down to the last book, I would have chucked it aside. But then there'd be no way to avoid my thoughts. Desperate, I doubled my focus and burrowed into the manic jargon of the story, hoping to lose sight of myself sooner rather than later.

[1]   I lay on the ground for hours, reading about Miller's relentless anxieties, before I heard Jarvis coming my way. His expression was carefully neutral and whatever he was thinking under his "BITE ME" ball cap remained concealed. His voice, though, had an urgency.

"Your buddy. Drone? That's his name?"

"Yeah. It's a nickname. Don't ask."

"Well, apparently he's been bit by a rattlesnake."

"What!?" That brought me fully upright.

"Yes, sir. Guess your guys made it into the gorge alright. I don't have all the details but seems that Drone flushed a snake hidden in the wall. Bit him on the hand; he definitely got a load of venom. Seems to be hanging in there, but the Navy chopper is coming in for an evac. We're getting him to the hospital ASAP."

"Jesus." My blood went cold. Drone! He had an intense phobia about snakes; crazy that he'd be the one to get bitten.

"Yes, sir. That's not all. George found your friend. Sorry to inform you that he is not alive. A fall, looks like," Jarvis paused a moment to let that sink in. "Drone was scouting an easier way out of the gorge so they could carry the remains. That's when he met the snake. Tough break. From what I hear there isn't any other way in or out, just the one your buddies used. Impressive, what they did. Gonna be a squeeze to get that chopper down in there far enough for a lift. But those Navy boys are good; if anybody can do it, it's them."

I nodded and Jarvis retreated with a promise to provide more updates. The information left me numb. We had our answer: Andy was dead. Well, no surprise there. The details would have to wait for George's account. I wasn't sure how much to worry about Drone. Rattlesnake bites aren't usually fatal, but it depends on how much toxin the snake injected. When a snake uses the toxin to kill prey, it is judicious about the amount. But if startled, or if the snake is young and inexperienced, it can unload its whole supply. Clearly, the rescue team didn't want to take chances. Well, that was good. If the fucking chopper didn't crash in the gorge trying to haul him out.

As I sorted through the news, it occurred to me that if I had kept going with the others, it could easily have been me instead of Drone. I knew more about the terrain and would have been a logical choice to scout. It was my thing. So, if I'd made it over the traverse, I would have been drilled by the snake. I obsessed about it. Even though the snake didn't bite me, I imagined what it must have been like: the sudden reptilian awareness, the searing pain with the strike, the rush of knowing what it meant, maybe death. My jaw clenched as I tried to contain these thoughts.

The sound of the Navy helicopter brought me to my feet. I walked over to the clearing where I could see the gorge. The big chopper had taken a position and hovered like a giant dragonfly. The noise was loud and insistent, washing down the slopes, echoing through the gorge and across the valley. The roar seemed palpable, like a creature of the wind. The chopper slowly dropped between the rock walls of Silver Creek. From where I stood the mission looked suicidal; I held my breath. Even a slight variance could push the blades up against the rock. I remembered how the small, bubble-dome chopper had bounced in the air currents. The Huey was a more stable ship, so they said, but the whole venture seemed precarious. I felt another spike of outrage over the risks taken for a corpse.

The chopper dropped out of sight, within the gorge, but I could hear it hovering. As long as I heard the steady thumping of the blades, I knew it was airborne and it was still a rescue, not an accident.

"You ever see those boys operate before?" Jarvis had crept up on me and I jumped in surprise.

"No, man."

"They run a tight op. A specialist goes down on a cable with a litter. He packages the victim on the litter. That gets reeled up into the ship and they send the cable back down for the specialist. Boys are fast and efficient. I saw them in Nam many times. A welcome sight, then and now."

I grunted, imagining the scene unfolding up in the gorge.

"One of your guys mentioned being in the Special Forces. Did you serve? If you don't mind me asking..."

"No. No, I didn't," which was all I was going to say about that.

We watched the Navy ship rise out of the gorge, amidst wild echoes and waves of shifting sound. Clear of the rock, the ship flew off down the valley, hospital bound.

"As soon as it drops Drone at the hospital in Fresno, it'll be back to lift out the remains." Jarvis was careful not to use Andy's name, perhaps a sign of respect, or a way to maintain a professional distance from death. But at this point, he was right, it was just remains. It wasn't Andy; Andy was dead.

I nodded to Jarvis and walked back to my tent. Nothing to do except read and wait for George and the gang.

It wasn't long before the chopper made its second run to get the corpse. This time the maneuver went more quickly. I guessed the pilot had learned what he needed to know. Then it was gone, down the valley.

I anesthetized myself with the ravings of Henry Miller until George, Tubbs, Carrot, and Ron came trooping back. They picked up ration boxes as they marched across the camp. When they got to our enclave, they threw themselves down on the ground in disarray. They looked drained. Tubbs broke the ice.

"What happened to you, compadre?"

"I dunno, man. I got to the traverse, and I just froze. I couldn't do it. Nerves, I guess. I dunno." I didn't see much point in trying to explain the tortured gymnastics of my head, even if I could have explained it.

"That's cool, man. Don't worry about it. Happens to all of us." Crazy Ron shared his combat wisdom, obviously trying to make me feel better. That I needed such tenderness only made me feel worse. No doubt about it, I was a loser. At least I wouldn't need to explain anything else. These guys accepted me already. I judged myself, fiercely, but my friends didn't. Or if they did, they kept it to themselves out of kindness or tolerance. We were all weird in our own ways and, to a certain extent, that's what made us unique. Quirks were prized possessions in this crowd, worn like scars and adornments.

I turned to George. "Tell me about Andy. Please."

"Sure. The gorge bends around a couple of times before it gets to that open area we saw in the flyover. It's a far-out place, almost circular, like a roofless chamber. The walls in there are hundreds of feet high so it feels like you're at the bottom of a giant well. It'd be amazing to go in there just to see it except... I never want to see it again. At the far end I found Andy." George paused for a moment, letting his thoughts come to order. "He was face down in a pool, pack smashed but still on his back. He was in pretty rough shape. Bloated; bruised; arms and a leg bent the wrong way. I didn't look any closer than I had to. The current had pushed him under an overhang, that's why we couldn't see him from above. No question that he fell over that cliff. Instant death. Looks like it was right below where we were the other day, where we saw that snake."

"Shit. Might as well blame the snake, then."

"Yeah. Andy was competent on rock; I don't think he would have slipped just because of the terrain. A startle, though... yeah, could be."

"Sorry, man. But it feels right that you found him. Not these cops."

"Yeah. Thanks."

If George was misty-eyed with the tale, I couldn't see it. It was getting dark, though. He looked away for a moment, then resumed opening cans of pound cake and assorted gruel and shoving big spoonfuls into his mouth.

It was quiet for a while, then Tubbs started in. "You should have seen the Drone, man, I thought he was gonna shit himself when that snake started chewing on him. He lets out a godawful shriek, then walks over to the rest of us with that old man hobble he does. He's white as a sheet and says in a whisper: 'Got me a snake tattoo.' I couldn't fuckin' believe it: 'Got me a snake tattoo!' That son of a bitch! Vintage Drone!"

We exploded in laughter. Ron couldn't restrain his glee. "Oh yeah, he was holding his hand like he'd just been shot, limping along, looking like death itself. High drama, my men, high drama."

Tubbs had more to say. "Well you know he's petrified of snakes. Never seen anybody so freaked about 'em. When we saw one in New Mexico he'd run away, squealing like a little girl, make everybody come over and kill it or chase it off. God, he drove everybody crazy."

"Some ironic justice, then, perhaps," observed Carrot, echoing my own thoughts on the matter.

"No doubt."

We laughed at Drone's histrionics and kept coming back to the topic. Fair game since he wasn't here—so what if he was in the hospital? Easier to talk about him than Andy, who was now nothing more than smashed remains in the morgue.

[m]   The next morning, I woke to Brad's best command voice. "Atten-shun!" He repeated it, slightly louder. I peered out the tent door and saw him standing at parade rest a few feet from our cluster of tents. Jarvis stood next to him, staring blankly into the trees. George, huddled in his bag, groaned and rolled over. From Tubbs' tent I heard something that sounded vaguely like "what's the rush motherfucker." Crazy Ron, the only one of us to have survived military service, responded with a clear and sarcastic, "Yes, sir!"

Nobody wanted to get up, but Brad and Jarvis waited us out, and eventually the whole crew of disheveled and disordered hippies stood in front of them. Having gotten the attention he wanted, Brad delivered a speech. "Alright, men, the first thing I want to do is say thank you for a job well done. You guys made it work. You showed us a thing or two about search and rescue. Yes, sir. Your skills made it possible to accomplish our mission, something that, I'm not too proud to admit, was beyond our means. So, thank you for that. Sorry about your buddy with the snakebite, but word I got from the hospital is that he is doing fine." He looked around as if waiting for applause or cheers, but the best he got was a couple of nods.

"So, gentlemen, we are done. The Huey is coming back at 0830 and will transport you all to the helipad. You best pack your gear and get it over to the clearing ASAP. I thank you again on behalf of the Fresno County Sheriff's Department for your service rendered. Be well, men." Brad saluted and marched off to get his team to work taking down the rope bridge and cleaning up their end of the camp.

Jarvis hung back for a few minutes, walking around and shaking everyone's hand. He didn't say anything, just smiled and nodded at each of us in turn. Of course, he had one of those bone-crushing handshakes that leave most folks writhing in pain. But climbers have strong hands, so he got as good as he gave. George even made him wince, just a fraction.

"Camp's fucked—let's bolt!" Tubbs called out the familiar New Mexico refrain that activated group exodus. If anyone uttered those words, even just the acronym "CFLB," it was a signal for everybody to leave. Once invoked, it had a peculiar binding effect. One of those nutty rituals that came out of nowhere. In this case, we were more than ready, and we jumped into action, taking down tents and jamming stuff into packs. Within a few minutes we were at the clearing. Crazy Ron and Tubbs were still eating pound cake, maybe because they couldn't fit any more cans in their packs and didn't want to abandon the booty.

I went through the motions but felt numb. To contain the bundle of shame and despair burning a hole in my gut, I had to smother it and pretend things were cool. Obviously, if I felt nothing on the surface, then I wouldn't feel the stuff I jammed down. That was my solution. The inner turmoil leaked out in unexpected words and acts, but it seemed a small price to pay for the immediate relief.

Soon the Huey could be heard coming up the valley. As it settled into the clearing, it looked gigantic compared to the little bubble-copter. We grabbed our packs and ran to the machine in a crouch, dragging our loads. Nobody wanted to risk getting a blade in the head. The crew helped us board through the large side port, which stayed open even in flight. There was a machine gun mount in the doorway, fortunately without a weapon, and an overhead boom where they cabled loads up and down. Loads like Andy and Drone. We sat on the floor, packs between our legs. Being last, as usual, I was closest to the open port. The view was stunning, but I kept thinking that if the ship tilted, I would slide right out. In some ways that would be a mercy, but I didn't really want to die. Once we were airborne, I appreciated the machine's stability and calmed down. It was too loud to talk, so I distracted myself by staring out the door and brooding.

The Huey was fast, and it wasn't long before we landed at the rescue staging area, back on the ridge where Pete had brought us only a few days ago. I felt disconnected from that experience, like it happened to someone else, no one I knew. As soon as we disembarked, the Huey took off and went back for the cops and their gear. With the chopper gone, the helipad was silent; we had it to ourselves.

We walked over to Drone's black and white Jeep Wagon parked next to the sheriff's rescue van. Tubbs had shown the foresight to get the keys from him before he was evacuated. He unlocked the wagon so we could load our packs, then he started checking the compartments on the van. I heard him chuckle.

"Hey hey hey. Check this out." He hoisted his prize: a half-case of Coors. "Ripe for the taking." He passed the beer to me and pulled out another half-rack. Ron and Carrot were over in a flash, checking the other bin panels. Some were locked, like the one containing the ropes, but Carrot found a couple of large bags of potato chips.

"I'd say this doesn't make us entirely even, but it's a start," smirked Tubbs.

"Yeah," I said, "now let's get out of here."

We drove away from the mountains, drinking cans of police beer and gobbling handfuls of potato chips. After a few days of backpacking food and C-rations, the chips tasted exotic, loaded with salt and grease and immediately satisfying. Our spirits ran high after ripping off the sheriff's department. The whole venture was another lark, I suppose, starting with the masquerade of pretending to be the Yosemite Search and Rescue team, on through showing up the cops at their own job, all the way to making off with their goodies in a trail of dust. Never mind that Drone was a sacrifice to the lark, he'd live. George laughed with the rest; wherever he stored his grief, it was deep. I suspected a reckoning awaited me as well, but I was free of the harsh wilderness and the clutches of the police and barreled down the open road with my friends, an escapee from purgatory. So, I acted giddy, laughing and swilling beer, plunging my hand into the chip bag, living the life. If there was grief of my own to feel, I wanted nothing to do with it.

We stopped at the Fresno hospital to visit Drone. As we walked through the ward and entered his room, it was evident from the sly smiles we got from the staff that Drone had been exercising his suave ways. He sat in a bed, propped with pillows and cloaked in the air of royalty, not bad for someone who had survived a primal phobia. No doubt the attentions of the nurses had helped to improve his state of mind. We crowded around his bed, slightly tipsy from all the beer, grinning at the reunion.

"Look at you, shithead, you're not even sick," said Tubbs.

"Awww, fuck you. That was one humongous snake. I could've died, no thanks to you maggots."

Ron stretched his arms in the air as one does to demonstrate the size of the fish that got away, then quickly shrunk them down to a two-foot span. "Yeah, man, humongous. About that big. Any smaller and it'd still be an egg."

"Fuck you, assholes. It hurt like a son of a bitch, that's all you need to know."

"More than the usual tattoo, I should imagine," Carrot observed. "Come on, show us." Drone lifted the gauze covering the back of his hand to display a grisly sight. His skin was black and red, puffed out as if ready to burst. It was obscene and made me sick to look at it. At that point a nurse swept in and admonished Drone to stop showing off while simultaneously shooing us out. As we left, Drone said he'd be there for a few more days. Tubbs promised that we'd send somebody back for him, but we were pushing on to Yosemite. Drone admitted that he was still working on a couple of the nurses, anyway.

We drove the rest of the way in silence, arriving in the Valley as if we'd returned from the moon. A lot of the climbers in Camp 4 wanted to know what happened down in King's Canyon, but I left that job to George. I set up the tent and crawled into my bag.

Sleep did not come quickly and when it did it brought a clear dream of falling over a never-ending cliff. As I fell, I went faster and faster. My skin burned and bits of flesh flew off, bit by bit, right down to the bone. Things went black and I woke, soaked with sweat, overheated in my sleeping bag. Throwing off the top, I gasped and trembled, trying to calm myself by thinking of other things. I couldn't focus on anything but burning. It took a long time to calm down and I spent the rest of the night on top of the bag, naked to the cool air.

[n]   Two days later Andy's parents arrived in the Valley. It was their nightmare to deal with the remains of their son. George talked with them on the phone before they came; he said that they wanted to learn about Andy's final days, and they asked to meet with us. Even in a funk, I couldn't refuse such a request. Mr. and Mrs. Cox took the two of us to lunch at a modest restaurant in Yosemite. I could tell they were torn between plying us with questions or explaining the depth of their loss. But they handled themselves with quiet dignity. I wondered if they blamed us for failing to save Andy, even if that meant saving him from himself. Their interest in us as representatives of Andy's world seemed genuine, not only as a desire to reach back into his life and vitality, but a way to honor his choices about that life.

During lunch, George told them the story of our trip, with a few comments from me. They liked George, as everyone did. His transparent integrity generated trust in people and Mr. and Mrs. Cox were no different. They also knew how important George was in Andy's world. Solid climbing partners are not that easy to find, and those two forged a team identity, one of the benefits of staying together through repeated adventures. Within that partnership, they envisioned a long future.

"You know, I taught him how to climb," Mr. Cox confessed. "We used to go to the local crags on Saturdays; it was our routine. We started when he was twelve. Already big for his age, restless, he had enough energy to consume the world. He didn't care for sports, but I could see he needed something physical, something to focus on. Climbing seemed perfect, and it was. He loved it; a light went on when he started climbing and then it was all he could think about. I loved our time together on the rocks. I felt inspired to see my son in his strength, finding his way up difficult routes, ones that I couldn't do. I was so proud of him."

What could we possibly say to that? Mrs. Cox took her husband's hand, and they sat in silence for a while, swaddled in their grief. I had never seen anyone openly accept such profound loss and I didn't know what to think. I had no room for grief; it seemed like a weakness to avoid. But I couldn't ignore the grace of the two parents. They were beautiful in sorrow, but it unnerved me, leading me to wonder if I lacked something. I already felt defective, anyway.

Mrs. Cox broke the silence and spoke while her eyes stared into space. "And on Sundays Andy and his father would sit and play chess for hours. Game after game. I loved to watch them so entranced with each other, so passionate in that way men have with their activities. I'd always make a batch of cookies just to keep them going... even after he got older and got involved with his friends, he still made time for the climbing and chess."

"I taught him to climb *and* to play chess," Mr. Cox acknowledged.

I had to say something. "Chess was how Andy and I met. A lot of climbers play chess, and we met over a game in Camp 4. We played a lot and got to know each other. Then Andy introduced me to George."

"Oh, really," Mr. Cox was intrigued. He thought for a moment. "Would you be interested in playing a game with me? For Andy's sake?"

"Sure. Of course, I would." I thought for a minute. "You know, Mr. Cox, Mrs. Cox, I don't really know how to say these things, but Andy was a really great guy. I don't know what to think about him being gone." There was more that I could have said and probably should have said but did not. If one more word escaped, it would pull me into realms of feeling that I was not prepared to divulge, to myself, or anyone. But I felt like I had to give them something, they were sublime in their sadness.

"Thank you, yes, we were proud of him."

Mr. Cox had a chess set with him, no accident I'm sure, so we walked from the restaurant to the edge of a meadow where a picnic table offered an opportunity to sit and play. From the table we had stunning views of Yosemite Falls in one direction and in the other the bulky bell-shaped massif of Cathedral Rocks and above that, soaring into the sky, the sheer tombstone tower of Sentinel Rock. A distracting vista, but once the board was unfolded and the pieces were in their places, I saw nothing but the squares. The conversation Mrs. Cox had with George at the other end of the table might have been on another planet. Mr. Cox played a decent game, but it wasn't long before I wiped him out. It didn't occur to me to play down to him or throw the game or any number of other options that might have compensated for his sadness. We were playing chess, the object was to win, and that was that. I didn't know any other way to be.

Mr. Cox grimaced as the game concluded. "Good game. I can see you know your way around the chessboard. Tell me, please, how did you do against Andy? I'd like to think I gave him a good start."

"I did okay. He was kinda reckless," I blurted out.

"Oh?" I saw Mr. Cox tense up and I regretted my stupid mouth.

"He loved the attack, he'd go all in. He stomped a lot of folks with wild combinations. They'd get dazed with sacrifices that he twisted into advantages—didn't know what hit 'em. But, you know, if you apply a defensive strategy..." I trailed off, hoping we could leave this subject.

"Yeah, yeah, that was Andy, wasn't it? Always charging in headfirst. In everything he did." Mr. Cox drifted into silence, staring absently down the valley at the granite towers. His expression promised tears, which I did not want to see, so I looked away and let my own thoughts fly far off into the distance.

The next day the Coxes held a wake for Andy in Camp 4. They bought several cases of beer and Pepsi and wanted anyone to attend who cared about Andy. We were all there, of course, George and me, Carrot, Tubbs, Crazy Ron and a couple dozen others who weren't off on the walls working on their climbing projects. Drone was still in the hospital, though we heard he would be released shortly. I thought the wake was a nice gesture, another attempt by Andy's parents to reach into his world and gather back some of his life. People drank the drinks and chatted intensely, which is the only way I've heard climbers converse. Everything was intense. George was able to joke and smile and the Coxs seemed content talking with the stalwarts of the vertical world. I spent the whole time by myself, leaning up against a giant pine tree, drinking beer, and staring into space. I felt thoroughly disconnected. I had slipped my social tether and fled, finding myself in a shadow world where I could barely make out the images of reality as if through an ashen veil. Every nerve in my body was frayed. I couldn't manage more than just existing.

Mr. and Mrs. Cox said goodbye and left after the wake. The next day they hired an airplane and flew over the Valley, scattering half of Andy's ashes. Then they turned south and flew to the Middle Fork of the King's River and scattered the other half over the Silver Creek gorge. The irony could have been a vindication, but it wasn't.

12

The Headwaters

I'd had enough of Yosemite and craved a refuge far away from the desiccated Sierra Nevada. Losing myself in the moist tangles of a rain forest sounded about right, and I packed my gear. Before parting, George and I made plans to go to Mexico in the fall, maybe as a way to move on without Andy. We shared a halfhearted farewell, and I hitchhiked north to Washington. Stopping in Seattle long enough to leave my climbing equipment with a friend, I hitched on to the Skagit Valley, walking and thumbing rides up progressively smaller roads until I arrived at an end. I'd been there before, the Baker River trailhead. It was a seldom-used trail that went a few miles up the river before fading into brush and old-growth forest. I went there with no expectations. I just wanted to go and sit beneath a giant cedar tree and breathe the soft air of the rain forest. Something cooked under my skin, down where I couldn't see it. I didn't know what to do about it, so I went to ground. Of course, I packed a book, but instead of escapist fiction I brought a tome by Sartre that I had meant to read for ages but had put off: *Being and Nothingness*. The title alone said everything: I was vacant, no being at all. I felt like nothing. Whether I read it or not, just carrying it around validated my predicament.

As I walked along the Baker River trail, I recalled my encounter with that wild landscape three years previously. It had been part of my first alpine adventure. The memory of the experience lingered within my conceit, and not in a good way. After learning to rock climb in New Mexico, as soon as I'd returned to the Northwest, I started scheming about the dramatic rock and ice of the North Cascades. I settled on a traverse of the Picket Range, a remote and formidable target. The route was complex and involved a sustained, multiday outing along jagged rock spires and hanging glaciers. Weather, rockfall, avalanches, and glacier travel all required special skills, of which I had virtually none. No matter. Other youth had hurled themselves at the alpine environment and even if they perished, they acquired nobility. Those that survived earned undying respect. Caught in my desires, as usual, I worked myself into a frenzy over the Picket traverse. Nothing could turn me back.

I recruited an old high school friend of mine who had some backpacking experience acquired from family outings and the Boy Scouts. Unfortunately, Jeff was in the early phase of schizophrenia. I had no understanding of that at the time, nor did anyone else that I knew. He was a little odd, but who wasn't in the late 60s? Jeff had no climbing experience, but I convinced him that we could handle the Pickets. All we needed were a couple of ice axes and a rope. Equipped with a few supplies and a minimum of gear, we had set off into the wilderness.

The approach, over twenty miles of trails and alpine paths, took longer than I anticipated and three days into the trip we ran out of food. At that point we were high up on Easy Ridge, a long, treeless spur of Whatcom Peak that provides access to the Pickets. Even my glory-seeking brain realized that we were not even going to get to the start of the traverse, let alone complete it. We studied the map and decided that we could descend directly from Easy Ridge into the Baker River drainage and follow the watercourse out to a trail that led to a road. It looked like the quickest way out of the mountains, shorter than reversing the long, tedious path we had taken to Easy Ridge. From our perch in the beautiful alpine meadows, I stared down into the mysteries of the Baker River, a thin ribbon far below, winding its way through an immense green valley. The slopes looked steep, but as far as I could see our descent would involve scrambling mostly through open meadowlands.

Once we started the descent, I saw my error. What had looked like meadows from above turned out to be a carpet of brush six feet deep. Thickets of slide alder forced us to crawl and bash our way forward. Trying to climb down the rock next to a waterfall, I slipped and lunged for a handhold. I stopped myself but broke a finger. I knew little about first aid but had packed Darvon in the kit because painkillers seemed like a good idea. I swallowed a couple of Darvon while Jeff used his Boy Scout knowledge to tape my fingers together as a splint. We pushed on because there was nothing else to do; we'd gotten far enough down the slope to not want to climb back up it. The descent to the valley floor was only a mile on the map; it took us most of the day. There was still daylight when the slope levelled off, so we kept going, but it didn't get easier. Jeff stumbled into a yellowjacket nest; he ran like hell and jumped in the river but still ended up with dozens of stings. Not long after that, we came to a small outcrop that had to be downclimbed or circumnavigated. Loaded and feeling no pain, I knew I could scramble down it in a jiffy. I grabbed a projecting root and swung over the face. The root broke and I plunged to the bottom of the cliff, then somersaulted backwards three times over the sharp-edged talus, coming to a crashing halt at the bottom. I had scraped all the skin off both shoulders, yet somehow my skull remained intact. We pushed on, following the riverbank, not understanding that's where the thickest brush grew. It took three days to cover the ten miles to the trail, eating wild blueberries as our only sustenance along the way.

By the time Jeff and I staggered onto the trail I didn't much care about the pristine surroundings, but the splendor of the cedar forest trickled into my memories anyway, lodging there like a dream. Later, I went back on a pilgrimage, hiking the trail just to camp alone under the old growth. I thought about Jeff. He talked about the trip as a great lark, but then he was crazy and getting worse every day. I only felt ashamed of my naivete; it had been an unnecessary ordeal. In the dark, lying on the ground, I tried to imagine that the whispers of the night were the voices of the trees, offering compassion for my many mistakes.

After Andy's death, as I swept through Seattle, I collected my mail. A letter from my mother said that Jeff had killed himself. He had been released from yet another hospitalization, a regular experience during the last two years as his psychosis intensified. His delusional symptoms abated, but not the depression. They judged him safe for the community anyway and sent him home.

In despair and without hope for his future, he put a plastic bag over the tailpipe of his car, sat behind the wheel, turned the ignition, and drifted away. I was stunned; it was too hard to understand. A surge of guilt left me feeling completely hollow. Before going to Tehipite with Andy and George I had received a letter from Jeff sent in care of general delivery at the Yosemite post office. In the letter he sounded defeated and apologized for his outrageous behaviors. My first thought had been "I don't have time for this shit." I failed to read between the remorseful lines of the letter, and I didn't respond, thinking I'd deal with it later. Now, there wasn't going to be a later.

Carrying the burden of these entwined complications, I walked up the Baker River and pushed on past the end of the trail. Far enough to be hidden, I set up my tent. Meandering around the forest, I placed my palms flat against the bark of the big old trees, hardly aware of what I was doing, just touching them because it seemed right. I couldn't shake off the haze of numbness. What the hell was wrong with me? Two good friends were dead, and I couldn't feel it. And more, there were the others from the last few years, those dead from overdose or car wrecks or any of the risky activities that we all accepted as the stuff of our days. I felt empty, a husk pretending to be a human. Not a climber, not a chess master, not anything. A pretender to friendship, someone who ignored the desperate pleas of a disabled friend, someone who could let a friend walk off to his death and feel nothing but anger, someone who was a coward instead of a hero. Waves of self-loathing rolled over me until I couldn't move. I dropped to my knees at the base of a giant cedar, curled up between the roots, and soon fell into a heavy sleep, too tired of myself to tolerate another moment.

I woke to a shift of the sun as it found my face through the branches. An onslaught of self-inspection started right away. The word "sacrifice" kept echoing in my thoughts. My only use of this concept was the gambit in chess, where a piece is offered to the opponent as bait. Should he or she accept the alluring sacrifice, it led to nasty combinations that often changed the course of the game. Sacrifice masked a trap. But as chess lore attests, the best refutation for a sacrifice is to accept it, dodge the trap, and expose the flaw in the opponent's plan. I was ill-prepared to comprehend other manifestations of sacrifice. Such things aroused my suspicion. Jeff's ultimate sacrifice, taking his own life, seemed pathetic. What was the point? I failed to see into the depth of his suffering and that, for him, the promise of life with psychosis was unbearable. It was not a game where he was seeking advantage, it was a game he wanted to end. So, he flipped over the board and scattered the pieces.

My anger at Andy was incomprehensible. That night on the slope above Silver Creek when the three of us were thirsty, irritated with each other, and full of gloom, he summoned the energy to run a couple of thousand feet down the hill and tote water for us. No small thing, heroic in essence, yet it might have sapped his reserves. Was his sacrifice a factor in the decision to leave us? Did his exhaustion contribute to falling over the cliff? Was that hard-earned water what killed him? It was a beautiful gesture, much appreciated, but we could have done without it. We weren't really going to die of thirst; we'd all experienced worse. It was a mean trick: he made a sacrifice for the water, which we accepted, then he ran off and got killed, leaving us the guilt.

In the branches overhead, I heard two ravens squawk at each other, back and forth in deliberation. I sat up and leaned back against the tree trunk. The afternoon sun sparkled off the cascades of the river while a breeze whispered through the dangling needles of the cedars. A deerfly landed on my arm and dug into the flesh. I swatted it away, but it came back, like they always do. This time I let it gnaw, relishing the pain. I deserved it. I wanted to be devoured by the world. Yet my mood was fickle, and I crushed the fly in my hand. Enough simple-minded nonsense: life could be harsh and marvelous, soft and sharp, an inscrutable mixture of possibilities, an arena for being, whether one wished to play the game or not. I was still a part of nature, entangled in its roots, and if I wanted to see my true self I had only to look around, for there I was, reflected with unnerving lucidity.

Automatically, I dug into the cargo pocket of my jacket and pulled out Sartre's book. In many ways, a man's lifework in a fat little paperback. What did it amount to, in the end? I was in no position to judge, being on trial myself.

I skimmed through the opening pages of perplexing jargon. It required headache levels of attention to wrap my head around the neologisms and their significance to a reader sitting under a tree in the mountains, grappling with despair. Flipping ahead, I suddenly emerged from the tangled syntax into a meadow of clarity, a section with the discomforting title "Bad Faith." As I read, phrases burrowed in and echoed through my skull.

I am sad. ...I am the sadness in the mode of being what I am. ...should we not say that being sad means first to make oneself sad? ... If I make myself sad, I must continue to make myself sad from beginning to end. ...in bad faith human reality is constituted as a being which is what it is not and which is not what it is. ...bad faith is not restricted to denying the qualities which I possess, to not seeing the being which I am. It attempts also to constitute myself as being what I am not. ...the first act of bad faith is to flee what it can not flee, to flee what it is. The very project of flight reveals to bad faith an inner disintegration in the heart of being, and it is this disintegration which bad faith wishes to be.

If I felt like a fraud, it's because I was. Layers of inauthenticity covered my soul, hiding it from the light of day. This was an old habit. I learned early that genuine emotions were not to be trusted. Make yourself vulnerable and you will pay. To distance myself from the core of feelings, I constructed masks of competence and detachment. Whatever I was at heart, whatever kind of being, I engaged in the project of pretending to be something else. This something else demanded thoughts and actions beyond my aptitude, leaving me with a schism, an anxiety-filled rift between truth and fantasy. No wonder that I craved escapism, no wonder that I fell into moods of paralysis. A being cannot function when it slices itself in pieces.

So, who was I, really? It hurt to see. I was someone who flew away from the untidy landscape of emotions, soaring, Icarus-like, into ethereal realms of abstract thinking: reading, chess, even climbing, physical enough but still, in essence, a mental game. And here I was still doing it, reading Sartre. How deluded can you get? I had tried to use the mechanistic powers of reason to wrestle things into order, applying layers on top of layers. Yet sustaining this mask required sacrifices, and entities of feeling, in a constant parade, were led to the altar and thrown into the maw.

Now the façade had cracked. Emotions crawled out of every cranny and demanded respect. I had no choice. It was time to look straight in the mirror. What I saw was not a philosopher, a grandmaster of the game, or a climbing machine. What I saw was a shy, sensitive boy, a bit touched, a bit of the poet. Whatever came next would have to follow from that.

I placed the book on the ground; I could read no more. A hummingbird arrived, materializing in that sudden way of their kind. It hovered in front of my eyes, then, abruptly as it came, it was gone. My heart flew with it as far as it could go. In an instant, the boundary between inner and outer dissolved, flowing together, blending into a river of being. I gazed across the tumbling water as it ran past, carrying its burdens downstream, headed for the sea. A tear rolled down my cheek. I hardly knew what it was. A trickle from the headwaters, maybe, from a source that threatened to never run dry.

ACKNOWLEDGMENTS

I am grateful to the late Irwin Klein for taking my photo amidst the craziness that was New Mexico in the late 60s and giving me a print, one of the few artifacts I've retained from that era. Irwin's nephew Benjamin Klein collected Irwin's New Mexico photos for the stunning book published by the University of Nebraska Press in 2016, *Irwin Klein and the New Settlers: Photographs of the Counterculture in New Mexico*. Readers are directed to this book to see portraits of some of the other denizens of *Wasted Youth*, all captured with Irwin's remarkable sense of character. Thumbing back and forth through the photos helped remind me of people, places, and events that had escaped my fumbling memories.

After discovering his book, I wrote to Ben Klein. He was kind enough to respond and we jumped into an energetic dialogue about hippies, the past, and Northern New Mexico. His input has been extremely helpful, and I can't thank him enough for his support.

I am also grateful for permission from Philippa Klein, Irwin's daughter, to use the photograph on the cover. I appreciate her kindness and interest in my work.

Both Richard Maiman and Christopher Ryan did yeoman's work in reading the text and offering useful suggestions. I am forever in their debt.

A big thanks to the Casco Bay Writers' Project at Mechanics' Hall in Portland for listening to me read my drafts over and over. Their keen ears and comments have been crucial.

Nowhere near least, even if last, has been the unwavering support of Susan T. Landry. She might not have liked me back in the 1960s, but I'm pleased that she likes me now.

The author lives with his dear wife in a creaky old house on the coast of Maine. He worked for thirty-five years as a psychotherapist specializing in family therapy and wilderness-based therapy. Before that he planted hundreds of thousands of trees in the industrial forest of the Pacific Northwest. During those years he lived off the grid, built log cabins, learned how to lay stone, and survived numerous exploits of mountaineering, rock climbing, and backcountry skiing. He is the author of two novels: *The Kraken Imaginary* (2022) and *Rhizome* (2021) winner of a Maine Literary Award. He's also published a collection of travel essays *Walking in Circles* (2023), and an extended essay in psychoecology, *Mirror of Beasts: Episodes of a Reflected Ecology* (2013). Website: www.wrightjamesm.com

The author on the Sheep's Head Peninsula, Ireland.
Photo by Susan T. Landry

www.ingramcontent.com/pod-product-compliance
Lightning Source LLC
LaVergne TN
LVHW061046070526
838201LV00074B/5194